# CAN WITCHCRAFT AFFECT CHRISTIANS

# CAN WITCHCRAFT AFFECT CHRISTIANS

## LIVING WITHOUT FEAR

Spiritual Warfare Series
Volume 8

Nellie Odhuno-Shani

Integrity
Publishers inc.

CAN WITCHCRAFT AFFECT CHRISTIANS: Living without Fear
Copyright © 2020 Nellie Odhuno-Shani

All Rights Reserved.

ISBN: 978-1-937455-35-4

Published by;

P.O. Box 58411,
Raleigh, NC 27658
U.S.A.
info@integritypublishers.org

Publishing Consultants:

info@publishing-institute.org
www.publishing-institute.org

All rights reserved. No portion of this book may be reproduced or transmitted in any form or by any means without the written permission of the author or Publisher.

# CONTENTS

| | | |
|---|---|---|
| | *Dedication* | vii |
| | *Introduction* | viii |
| 1 | The Origin of Witchcraft | 1 |
| 2 | God's View on Witchcraft | 6 |
| 3 | How Witchcraft Works | 10 |
| 4 | Black Witchcraft | 17 |
| 5 | Witchcraft and Blood Covenants | 24 |
| 6 | Areas touched by Witchcraft | 29 |
| 7 | People likely to use Witchcraft | 43 |
| 8 | White Witchcraft | 52 |
| 9 | How safe are you? | 60 |
| 10 | Ensuring our Safety | 66 |
| | *About the Author* | 71 |
| | *Other Books by Author* | 72 |

# Dedication

This book is dedicated to the Holy Spirit, the sole administrator of God's estate! It is He who hovered over the waters in Genesis when the earth was formless and empty, and darkness was over the surface of the deep. He is the third Person of the Trinity, having equal power and status with God the Father, and God the Son. It is He who comes into a Believer at salvation. The apostle John said of Him **"But the Counsellor, the Holy Spirit, whom the Father will send in my name, will teach you all things and will remind you of everything I have said to you."** As the Spirit of Truth He guides us into all truth and does not speak on His own. He speaks only what He hears, and tells us of what is yet to come. He brings glory to God by taking what belongs to God and reveals it to us. He alone reveals the mind of God. He takes deep secrets, things hidden at the foundation of the world and reveals it to us. He convicts of sin, righteousness and judgment. To Him be honour and praise forevermore!

# Introduction

My earliest contact with witchcraft was in cartoons. If anyone said the word "Witchcraft", I would conjure up in my young mind, a night scene with a black castle and bats flying around it. Also flying around it, on a broom, would be a very thin woman dressed in black. She wore a pointed hat, and whenever her face (It was always a woman) came close enough for us to see it, she had a long hooked nose with huge pimples on it. She had a wicked smile, revealing a missing front tooth! Witchcraft and witches were a fairy tale, told to children when we wanted them to obey. "Eat your food quickly, or a flying witch is going to come to your bedroom at night!"

While a lot of people from the West have grown up believing that witchcraft is simply a figment of people's imagination (greatly aided by movies from Hollywood), many people from Third World countries have seen a lot of misfortune around them that have been attributed to the power of witchcraft. In Kenya my home country, people especially in the villages, often blame witchcraft as the root cause of death, accidents, sickness, poverty, insanity and family strife.

Among the affluent however, witchcraft is seen as "village superstition," not worth paying attention to. Despite the common notion that belief in witchcraft is rife among the poor and downtrodden villagers, a quick ride through the streets of the cities paints a different picture all together. Posters pasted on lamp posts advertise diviners, whose services include love portions to make a person fall in love with you, barren women being able to get children, how to get a dream job, and how to protect yourself from your enemies, just to name a few.

So what is the truth about witchcraft? Is it something I should ever have sleepless nights over? How real is it? Will I be affected if someone looks at me with the "Evil eye?" As I have had opportunity to interact with various people in different countries (My husband, our children and I have lived in six different countries, on three different continents), I have met many people who say that they do not believe in witchcraft. Others say witchcraft exists, but will only affect you if you believe in its power. It is interesting to note that these beliefs are found among both Christians, and non-Christians alike. They have hence brushed off the topic as one would brush off an irritating fly that is perched on their shoulder!

This book will not give you complete knowledge and answers to all your questions about witchcraft. However, it attempts to bring to the light, all that the Bible has revealed about witchcraft. Deuteronomy 29:29 says *"The secret things belong to the Lord our God, but the things revealed belong to us and to our children forever, that we may follow all the words of this law."* The Bible is not a flippant book, but was written by men, inspired by the Holy Spirit. Apostle Paul, in a bid to draw his disciple Timothy to the importance of the Word of God, told him in 2 Timothy 3:16-17, *"All scripture is God-breathed and is useful for teaching, rebuking, correcting and training in righteousness, so that the man of God may be thoroughly equipped for every good work."* I recognise the Word of God as the final authority on all matters, so this book leans solely on the Bible for all knowledge and answers to this interesting and important topic. Let the Word of God equip us concerning witchcraft.

Contrary to what many people think, witchcraft is talked about in the Bible. It is therefore prudent to study the Word of God, to know whether witchcraft is real or not, and if it is, how to live a life free from its effects.

Chapter one

# The Origin of Witchcraft

The dictionary calls witchcraft, the practice of black magic involving the supposed invocation of evil spirits for evil purposes. It uses spells and the invocation of spirits. It is the power of apparently influencing the course of events by using mysterious or supernatural forces.

From the dictionary definition above, witchcraft is a person invoking evil spirits using spells to influence the course of events for evil purposes. The only person that the Bible says has come to steal, kill and destroy is Satan. Those are all evil purposes. Jesus said speaking of Satan in John 10:10, *"The thief comes only to steal, kill and destroy; I have come that they may have life and have it to the full."* So whoever kills, or destroys, is in league with Satan. The bottom line is that anyone involved in witchcraft is an employee of Satan and his evil forces, and is working to advance the agenda of the "dark world". Satan hates mankind because they are made in the image of God. The second and very compelling reason why Satan hates human beings is because they replaced him in the Garden of Eden! He was simply driven by intense jealousy when he approached Eve and tempted her to disobey God so that they would be thrown out of the Garden. Let us hear what Ezekiel 28:13-14 about of where Satan was before he was kicked out from God's presence. *"You were the model of perfection, full of wisdom and perfect in beauty. You were in Eden, the Garden of God; every precious stone adorned you…"* Each time Satan sees a human being, it reminds him of his fall and replacement! No human being should ever believe the lie, that he is their friend. Satan hates us all with a perfect hatred! Even when he uses witchdoctors to accomplish his purposes, his desire is to finally destroy them. The Bible tells us that after Satan rebelled against God he was kicked out of heaven.

> *"How you have fallen from heaven O morning star, son of the dawn! You have been cast down to the earth… you said in your heart, 'I will ascend to heaven; I will raise my throne above the stars of God; I will sit enthroned on the mount of assembly, on the utmost heights of the sacred mountain. I will ascend above the tops of the clouds; I will make myself like the Most High.'"*
>
> Isaiah 14:12-14.

Looking at these verses in Isaiah, it is quite obvious that the sin that got Satan kicked out of heaven was pride. Satan refused to submit to the authority of God. In witchcraft, people refuse to submit to the authority of God as they are driven by pride. Satan's main aim of stealing, killing and destroying is against men and women, who are made in the image of his enemy – God. When Satan was kicked out of heaven, he landed on earth.

> *"And there was war in heaven. Michael and his angels fought against the dragon, and the dragon and his angels fought back. But he was not strong enough, and they lost their place in heaven. The great dragon was hurled down – that ancient serpent called the devil, or*

*Satan, who leads the whole world astray. He was hurled to the earth, and his angels with him."*

Revelation 12:7-9.

We need to understand that the battle was not between God and Satan. It was between Satan and the Archangel Michael. The Bible says, **"But he was not strong enough, and they lost their place in heaven."** Satan could not defeat the Archangel Michael. How then can he hope to defeat God? As we study the topic of witchcraft, we must understand that God is infinitely stronger than Satan. There can be no comparison! How can a pot fight with the potter? How can the basket rebel against the one who weaved it? It is utterly ridiculous to imagine that Satan has the same power as God.

There is a warning that the inhabitants of the earth are given in Revelation 12:12. **"Therefore rejoice, you heavens and you who dwell in them! But woe to the earth and the sea, because the devil has gone down to you! He is filled with fury, because he knows that his time is short."** The devil that was cast down to the earth is filled with fury. Satan knows better than anybody else that his end will be in the Lake of fire (Revelation 20:10). However, while he is on earth, his aim is to fight mankind and kill and destroy as many people as he can before his final destruction!

Because Satan and his angels are spirits, they cannot operate on the earth without bodies. Satan needs human agents with whom to work to accomplish his wicked schemes against mankind. Satan knows that a human-being is born sinful. All he needs to do is to manipulate that evil human nature for his purposes. Listen to what God said about human beings that He had created. **"The Lord saw how great man's wickedness on the earth had become, and that every inclination of the thoughts of his heart was only evil all the time."** – Genesis 6:5. Man's wickedness works to Satan's advantage!

Eve ate the forbidden fruit because she was power hungry. She wanted to be like God, knowing good and evil. Adam and Eve were kicked out of the garden for the same reason that Lucifer (Satan) was kicked out of heaven. It was a lust for power! This same lust for power and recognition is the same reason that people become witchdoctors! – In this book, the term "witchdoctor" will be used for both men and women.

Satan lures human agents by offering them power to control and manipulate people and circumstances. Show me a witchdoctor, and I will show you someone who was lured by his or her quest for power. What witchdoctors do not realize is that although they work for Satan, he is not their friend. Satan will use them to steal people's wealth, health, destroy them, and then turn around and destroy the witchdoctor! Satan is only full of hatred and is incapable of loving.

At its foundation, witchcraft is the worship of Satan. There are only two spiritual forces in the universe – God and Satan. God is the Creator of the whole universe while Satan is a created being. We see Lucifer (Satan) as a created being in Ezekiel 28: 14-15 **"You were anointed as a guardian cherub, for so I ordained you. You were on the holy mountain of God; you walked among the fiery stones. You were blameless in your ways from the day you were created till wickedness was found in you."** Satan is like the proverbial pot that tries to fight the potter! The basket that thinks he is able to fight the weaver!

## PRAYER

Heavenly Father, thank you for teaching me about the origin of witchcraft. Forgive me for thinking that witchcraft is not real, or that if I ignore it, then it will not affect me. I yield myself to You to continue teaching me what Your Word says about this subject. I have realized that the origin of witchcraft is Satan, and that You are infinitely more powerful than Satan. Forgive me for lusting for power in any area of my life. Thank you for showing me that when I lust for power, then I open myself up to Satan's seductions. I renounce and denounce any lust for power in my life. I believe that You are the only One and true God. I desire only You! As I read this book, remove from me, any wrong perceptions that I hold concerning witchcraft. I will no longer be prey to the devils lies. I now take authority and command any spirit of false belief concerning witchcraft to leave me now in the name of Jesus Christ! **Spirits of deception, skepticism and rationalization**, leave me now in Jesus name! Breathe out through your mouth. In Jesus name I pray – Amen!

Chapter Two

# God's View on Witchcraft

Although the Bible mentions sorcerers in many passages of the Bible, before this incident we don't hear God speaking directly against them. The first time that we see God's displeasure towards sorcery and witchcraft is in the story of Balaam the witchdoctor. We find the story in the twenty- second and twenty-third chapters of the book of Numbers. In this story the Israelites had come out of Egypt and had started conquering the kings in the land of Canaan. When they reached Moab, and camped just outside the land, this brought real terror to the Moabites. *"Now Balak son of Zippor saw all that Israel had done to the Amorites, and Moab was terrified because there were so many people. Indeed, Moab was filled with dread because of the Israelites."* – Numbers 22:2-3.

Balak was the king of Moab and he knew that there was no way that he could defeat the Israelites if he engaged them in a face -to -face battle. He decided that rather than be defeated in a physical encounter with this intimidating enemy, he would engage the services of someone who would help them win in a spiritual encounter! He decided to reach out for help from Balaam the witchdoctor. King Balak called for Balaam because his powers had already been proven. Here is the message that he sent to the witchdoctor. *"Now come and put a curse on these people, because they are too powerful for me.*

*Perhaps then I will be able to defeat them and drive them out of the country. For I know that those you bless are blessed, and those you curse are cursed."* - Numbers 22:6. After the people that the king had sent to Balaam brought him the message, God said to him, *"Do not go with them. You must not put a curse on those people, because they are blessed."* God intervened on behalf of Israel and rebuked the witchdoctor.

When my family lived in the West African country of Senegal, a pastor told me how a witchdoctor who someone had asked to curse him refused to do so. The witchdoctor told his client who happened to be his mother, that he was unable to curse her son. This mother wanted her son cursed for shaming the family by becoming a believer in Jesus Christ, converting from his family religion of Islam. He told her that he could see light surrounding her son and that God would not let him curse the young man. This mother later gave her life to Jesus Christ as a result of this encounter with the witchdoctor.

In Exodus 22:18 God told the Israelites, **"Do not allow a sorceress to live."** We need to understand that in the Old Testament there was no mercy or grace. The immediate judgment on witches and wizards was instant death by stoning! This was the law that God gave to Moses concerning witchcraft. *"For the law was given through Moses; grace and truth came through Jesus Christ."* – John 1:17. Today witchdoctors are not stoned to death because Jesus Christ, through His death on the cross of Calvary, brought about mercy and grace. Any witchdoctors reading this book should be grateful that because of the shed blood of Jesus Christ, instant stoning has not been meted out on him or her. But if they do not turn away from witchcraft and give their lives to Christ, they will end up in the Lake of Fire on the Day of Judgement.

Sorcery and witchcraft are closely related. Sorcery is the use of black magic. Witchdoctors use sorcery to control and manipulate their subjects. In Leviticus 20:27, God again shows His hatred of witchcraft. **"A man or woman who is a medium or spiritist among you must be put to death. You are to stone them; their blood will be on their own heads."** Witchdoctors consider themselves as mediums. They claim to be able to connect the living and the dead, getting their instructions from spirits. Although none of them will admit that they contact evil spirits, any spirit that is not the Holy Spirit of God is an evil spirit regardless of the "good deeds" that they claim to do. I remember a witchdoctor (who had turned away from witchcraft) who told me that she used good spirits to destroy bad spirits. What deception! Evil spirits are servants of Satan and their only purpose is to do their master's will, which is to steal, kill and destroy! We need to understand that there are no good spirits.

As the Israelites were beginning to take over the land of Canaan, God warned them. **"When you enter the land the Lord is giving you, do not learn to imitate the detestable ways of the nations there. Let no one be found among you who sacrifices his son or daughter in the fire, who practices divination or sorcery, interprets omens, engages in witchcraft, or casts spells, or who consults the dead. Anyone who does these things is detestable to the Lord…"** – Deuteronomy 18:10-12. Anyone who practises witchcraft is detestable to the Lord! As I have counselled Christians I have encountered many of them who have gone to see witchdoctors when they have waited "long enough" for the Lord to come through for them in a certain area of their lives and have been "disappointed by the Lord." When I have asked them whether they eventually got what they had been waiting for after going to consult the witchdoctor, the answer has always been "no". Witchcraft is a deception that Satan has used to trap many people into a web of suffering and disappointment. I praise God that no matter how many times a person has gone to see witchdoctors, when they turn to Jesus Christ in true repentance, He is always ready to forgive their sins and cleanse them with His blood! – 1 John 1:9.

# God's View on Witchcraft

The full extent of God's hatred of witchcraft, which in essence is worshipping another god, is seen in Deuteronomy 5:7-9. ***"You shall have no other gods before me...for I, the Lord your God, am a jealous God, punishing the children for the sin of the fathers to the third and fourth generation of those who hate me."*** When it comes to witchcraft, God will punish children, grandchildren and great grandchildren because of the sin of their fathers. Lamentations 5:7 says, **"Our fathers sinned and are no more and we bear their punishment."** God hates witchcraft and will not spare anyone who practices it! He told Israel in Micah 5:12, **"I will destroy your witchcraft, and you will no longer cast spells."**

## PRAYER

Heavenly Father, thank you for showing me how much You hate witchcraft. I now understand that witchcraft brings punishment on four generations, even on those people who did not practice it directly. Forgive me and cleanse me with the blood of Jesus Christ for any witchcraft that I, or my forefathers have practised either knowingly or unknowingly. Let me have the same hatred for witchcraft that You have dear God. In Jesus name I pray – Amen!

Chapter Three

# How Witchcraft Works

Ephesians 6:10 exhort us to **"Put on the full armor of God so that you can take your stand against the devil's schemes."** To scheme is to make plans in a devious way or with an intention to do something wrong. Witchcraft is one of Satan's schemes and it will do us well to know how it works. Unfortunately I learned the hard way, how witchcraft works.

I was newly married and our first –born son was not yet two years old. An elderly lady had come to visit me and brought me a gift of green peas. After she left, my house-help came to me carrying a small black "thing" in her hands. She told me that she had found that small black thing in the peas and that the lady who had just visited us was using witchcraft on me. I examined the "thing", and it looked like a burned piece of fat. I told her to throw it away and dismissed the theory of someone trying to use witchcraft on me. I told her to go ahead and cook the peas. She cooked the peas and we ate it. That same evening my son fell down while running and got badly injured. I had to take him to hospital where he got four stitches as a result of a cut on his forehead. While the doctor was stitching the cut on my son's forehead I fainted. I never connected the events of the evening with the peas that had the black "thing" in it. It was only a few years later in retrospect, and when I learnt about how witchcraft works, that I realised that the elderly lady had actually tried to harm my family through witchcraft. Why the witchcraft worked on us yet I was a believer, will be discussed is a later chapter.

In Ezekiel 13:18-23, we see God telling the prophet Ezekiel how witchcraft works on His people.

## PROPHESYING

To prophesy is to say with confidence that something is going to happen in the future. Here we are not dealing with prophesying as relates to God, but prophesying as relates to witchdoctors. In Ezekiel 13:17 God tells the prophet how prophecy works in witchcraft. ***"Now, son of man, set your face against the daughters of your people who prophesy out of their own imagination."*** Many witchdoctors are often seen as prophets. They claim to be able to tell you what will happen in the future. The interesting fact is that many of the things that witchdoctors tell people actually happen! A certain woman told me that a witchdoctor told her that there was going to be a death in the family and it actually happened. She asked me how come the prophecy came to pass. I told her that Satan does not know the future but can make things happen. All that the witchdoctor did when he prophesied that someone was going to die, was simply to send the spirit of death to go and kill someone in that family. Since Proverbs 26:2 says, ***"...An undeserved curse does not come to rest,"*** the person who died must have had a valid reason in their life, why the spirit of death had the legal right to kill them. So we can see that a prophecy from a witchdoctor is simply an assignment for an evil spirit to accomplish what they have said will happen. If a witchdoctor prophesies that an accident is going to happen, then an evil spirit will go and cause the accident to happen. This often gives the false impression that witchdoctors know what is going to happen in the future. Only God knows what is going to happen in the future. God told Ezekiel that the daughters of Israel prophesied out of their own imagination. Witchdoctors simply imagine things then send evil spirits to accomplish what they have imagined. Be warned that not all prophecy is from God, even if what was prophesied comes to pass!

## ENSNARING

To ensnare is to catch as in a trap. When I was growing up, I often saw my father set out a trap to catch mice. They were often put in the granary where dried maize and beans would be stored. My dad would put some food inside the trap. As soon as the rodent entered the trap to get the food, some metal rod triggered by the weight of the mouse would come down and clamp on to its head. Many times in the morning we would find the creature ensnared by the trap – dead. God went on to describe to Ezekiel, what these women witchdoctors were doing. *"...This is what the sovereign God says: Woe to the women who sew magic charms on all their wrists and make veils of various lengths for their heads in order to ensnare people. Will you ensnare the lives of my people but preserve your own?"* – Ezekiel 13:18. Israel in the Old Testament represents born-again believers today (Read John 3:1-3 to understand why Christians are called born-again). The Israelites were the people of God. So when God says that these women witchdoctors were ensnaring the lives of His people, it is the same as saying that believers in Christ are being ensnared!

Agatha (not her real name) came to see me for some counsel, after being ensnared by a witchdoctor posing as a man of God. She was a deacon in a Baptist church and hardly looked like the kind of woman that could be ensnared. After having been overlooked for a promotion three times at her place of work, Agatha decided to share her frustration with an office colleague. Her colleague suggested that she take her to see a man of God who would pray for her and resolve her problem. Agatha had no reason to suspect the man that her colleague took her to see. Contrary to how many people recognise witchdoctors, this man was not in a dark room surrounded by gourds, chicken skulls, and dried goat -skin. On the contrary he lived in a middle-class residential area, and wore jeans and a tee shirt. Agatha's guard immediately went down as the man removed a Bible and set it on the small table next to him. Next he brought a basin of water and placed it in front of Agatha. The scene of Jesus washing His disciples feet flashed through her mind, only that instead of a foot washing ceremony, he asked her to look into the water. Without thinking, Agatha looked into the water and saw a letter lying at the bottom of the shallow basin. He asked her to take it out of the water. Agatha removed a dripping piece of paper out of the basin. He asked her to read it. The letter was addressed to someone called "Mzee". The writer was telling Mzee that he needed a charm that was strong enough that if he put it in Agatha's office, she would eventually fall sick and die! He also told Mzee that he had sent him 20,000 Kenya shillings and was going to send the balance once he received the charm. Agatha was understandably shaken! The "Man of God" told Agatha not to worry and that he was going to pray to nullify the power of Mzee's charm. However, since the charm cost over 20,000 Kenya shillings, Agatha was going to have to pay double the money for his prayer to cancel the power of the charm. He asked Agatha how much money she had on her and she said that she only had 5,000. Agatha produced it and he quickly pocketed it. The "Man of God" opened the Bible to the book of Psalm and read something about how God protects His children. He gave her a crumpled piece of paper tied up with a red piece of string representing the blood of Jesus. She was to keep this in her handbag at all times! He also made

Agatha promise that the balance of 35,000 Kenya shillings would be sent to him within the next three weeks.

It was only after Agatha got back to her house that she realised what had just happened. She had just been to see a witchdoctor! Shame and fear like she had never experienced in her life before gripped her! The very next day Agatha received three calls from the "Man of God" which she did not pick up. Within the next week the "Man of God called her at least twenty times. Agatha developed high blood pressure and started having nightmares. Even after blocking his number, the "Man of God's" calls continued to come through! She realised that she was dealing with something very demonic! It was in this state that Agatha reached out for help. How was Agatha to get out of this unfortunate predicament? Joel 2:32 tell us ***"And everyone who calls on the name of the Lord will be saved; for on Mount Zion and in Jerusalem there will be deliverance..."***

Because Agatha was a believer in Jesus Christ, she could call upon Jesus to help and deliver her! All that was required was for Agatha to accept guilt for going to see a witchdoctor even though she was unaware of it. Next she needed to ask God to forgive her and have mercy on her. After that she needed to ask Jesus Christ who is her Advocate (1 John 2:1), for cleansing through His blood. She would then ask God who is the Righteous Judge to give her a verdict of "Not guilty." It was only after these steps that Agatha would need to break an ungodly soul tie with "Man of God" and cast out the evil spirits that entered her. They would typically be spirits of witchcraft, divination, fear, worry, compromise and any other spirits that the Holy Spirit brings to her mind. Jesus warned His disciples in Mathew 24:24, ***"For false Christs and false prophets will appear and perform great signs and miracles to deceive even the elect – if that were possible."*** We need to understand that witchcraft works through deception, and it is evil spirits who carry out the witchdoctor's spoken curses and incantations. Witchdoctors also often use charms, which they give their clients for protection. Charms invite the presence of evil spirits. Deuteronomy 7:26 says, *"Do not bring a detestable thing in your house or you, like it, will be set apart for destruction. Utterly abhor and detest it for it is set apart for destruction."* The charm that the elderly lady put in the peas that she brought to me, invited the presence of evil spirits into my house. It was an evil spirit that caused my son to fall and hit his head against the edge of the chair.

Agatha judged the "Man of God" by his outward appearance and the fact that he had a Bible, and was ensnared. However even if we have been ensnared, all is not lost. Listen to what God tells the witchdoctor. *"Therefore this is what the sovereign God says: I am against your magic charms with which you ensnare my people like birds. I will tear off your veils and save my people from your hands, and they will no longer fall prey to your power. Then you will know that I am the Lord."* – Ezekiel 13:20. Witchdoctors have power, only it is power given to them by Satan. Agatha fell prey to the power of the "Man of God," who used demonic power to lure her. God also said, *"Because you disheartened the righteous with your lies, when I had brought them no grief…therefore you will no longer see false visions or practice divination. I will save my people from your hands. Then you will know that I am the Lord."* – Ezekiel 13:22-23. Agatha was disheartened and full of grief when she was told that her boss wanted her dead! The "Man of God" was seeing a false vision and practising divination. However what a loving God we have! When we have been ensnared and deceived, He promises to save us from that deception if we will turn to Him in repentance.

## PRAYER

Heavenly Father, thank you for showing us some of the ways that witchcraft works. Thank You for Your Word, which says that He who is in us is far greater than he who is in the world. Forgive me for any time that I have unknowingly gone to see anyone who uses demonic power to control people. I cancel any false prophecy that has ever been said over me by anyone using demonic power in the name of Jesus Christ! I declare that I will not be ensnared through witchcraft in Jesus name! Thank you for being my deliverer from the powers of witchcraft. I command spirits of witchcraft and deception to leave me in the name of Jesus Christ. I declare that I am set free in Jesus name!

Chapter Four

# Black Witchcraft

People who are officially called witchdoctors practice a trade called black witchcraft. They carry out their practice in specific places so that their clientele can locate them when they need their services. The typical witchdoctor often has a room where they practice their craft. The room is often dark, and has a lot of paraphernalia. In most countries in Africa, these items will often consist of animal skulls, bones, gourds, bowls, bird feathers, cowrie shells, dirty looking bottles of various sizes, dirty pieces of cloth, candles in various colours and sometimes even an old looking Bible!

From conversations with people who have solicited the services of witchdoctors, I have gathered that fear is the first emotion that they feel as they walk into the small dark room. One person told me that it was almost pitch dark in the room although outside the sun was shining brightly. Proverbs 4:19 says, *"But the way of the wicked is like deep darkness; they do not know what makes them stumble."* Only the wildest imagination can perceive what a person can stumble upon in the dark room of a witchdoctor!

The stereo- type image of a witchdoctor is often of an old or aging man or woman whose clothes are often not very clean. A torn dirty curtain covering the window and utensils strewn on the floor, will greet us as our eyes become accustomed to the darkness. A similarly dirty curtain often shields off a mysterious area from where the witchdoctor will supposedly converse with spirits of the dead. It is in such places that very intelligent and smartly dressed people sit on the floor to inquire about their fate and perceived enemies! It is also from the dirty bottles that mysterious liquids are given to clients to drink. It is interesting to note that people leave their manicured gardens and clean houses to go to "get help" from witchdoctors - A person advising them on how to get rich, while living in a dirty old dilapidated house!

A "Black Witch" serves Satan. They use demonic powers to control and manipulate people. A person wanting to cast an evil spell on their enemy will typically solicit the services of a witchdoctor who will use black witchcraft to accomplish his purpose. Black witchcraft involves the use of incantations, spoken curses and charms. The main aim is to inflict poverty, sickness, madness and even death on their victims. Love portions are also part of black witchcraft. These portions are often used to get a person to love somebody against their will.

Black witches use fear, the love of money, and the lust for power, to ensnare and control their subjects. The Bible tells us that the love of money is the root of all evil (1 Timothy 6:10). One of the evils of the love of money is that it drives people to the doorstep of witchdoctors. Fear of losing one's life, children, lover, or property would rank the highest in the reasons why people subject themselves to the control of witchdoctors. We all know that word of mouth is one of the most effective marketing strategies that exist. It is for this reason that many people who have gone to see witchdoctors have often been advised to do so by a friend or relative. We see a warning in Isaiah 8: 19 **"When men tell you to consult mediums and spiritists, who whisper and mutter, should not a people inquire of their God? Why** *consult the dead on behalf of the living?* The implication here is that it is ridiculous to consult people who could not keep themselves alive, to give us advice on how to stay alive! Witchdoctors claim to hear instructions from spirits of people who have already died. Why do I say that they **claim** to hear? This is because nobody who has already died has any right to come back to the earth to talk to the living. Many times I have wondered whether witchdoctors are deliberately deceiving people, or whether they truly believe that they are communicating with the dead. Hebrews 9: 27 says *"Just as man is destined to die once, and after that to face judgment."* After death the only thing that a person faces is judgment. In the book of Job we read, *"But man dies and is laid low; he breathes his last and is no more. As waters disappear from the sea or a riverbed becomes parched and dry, so man lies down and does not rise; till the heavens are no more, men will not awake or be roused from their sleep."* If dead people cannot be roused from their sleep then who is it that witchdoctors communicate with? Witchdoctors communicate with **evil spirits of divination** masquerading as dead people!

The Bible in the book of Acts chapter 16:16-18, give us an account of Paul and Silas' encounter with a slave girl who had a spirit by which she predicted the future. We are told that she earned a great deal of money for her owners by fortune- telling. Why did fortune-telling bring in a lot of money? It is because a lot of people are interested in knowing what will happen to them in the future. Satan takes advantage of this desire to deceive people through his agents. The slave girl was an agent of Satan. To try and ensnare Paul and Silas, Satan knew that he had to first gain their confidence. Only the truth would make Paul's guard go down so the spirit of divination said through the girl, *"These men are servants of the Most High God, who are telling you the way to be saved"* – Acts 16:17. Paul was not able to detect immediately that this girl was using the spirit of divination because she was speaking the truth. We are told that she kept this up for many days. Because this was a spirit of divination, Paul's spirit was disturbed although he probably did not know why this was so. We are told, **"Finally Paul became so troubled that he turned around and said to the spirit. 'In the name of Jesus Christ I command you to come out of her!' At that moment the spirit left her."** – Acts 16:18. It was only the intervention of the Holy Spirit speaking to Paul's spirit that discerned for Paul the true nature of this spirit! Many Christians are unaware that demons can speak the truth. However that truth is supposed to make way for the lie! Whenever our spirit is troubled, we should stop what we are doing and inquire of the Holy Spirit to discern for us what we are dealing with. There are many people who I have counselled who have told me that their spirit was troubled when they were introduced to a "Man of God" or a "Woman of God" yet there was nothing that they could put their finger on as to what wrong the person had done. They therefore ignored the warning sign. Many times the way that the Holy Spirit warns us is by causing our spirit to be troubled.

Once the spirit of divination left the slave girl, she could no longer foretell the future. It was the demon within her that had been telling people about their future. Witchdoctors foretell the future using an evil spirit of divination and not spirits of dead people!

It seems like witchdoctors use different methods to curse and put spells on people, depending on where they come from. People I have talked to, who have gone to see witchdoctors in East Africa, have told me very different things from people who went to see witchdoctors in West Africa. When my family lived in a country in West Africa, we were not aware that our landlord was using witchcraft on us. It was a period in my life when the Lord was teaching me a lot on spiritual warfare and I am convinced that the reason why God allowed us to go through this experience was to teach me one of the ways that people use witchcraft to control.

We moved into a house with a big compound, with three beautiful mature trees growing in the backyard. Our designated prayer room was right above the garden in the two- storey house. At that time I had just learned that we needed to pray that, any planting which was not of the Lord in our compound, be uprooted in the name of Jesus Christ! The verse that inspired this prayer was Matthew 15:13 ***"Every plant that my heavenly Father has not planted will be pulled up by the roots."*** A few months after moving into our home, we noticed that one of the big leafy trees was beginning to dry up. My husband bought some manure and asked our gardener to put it in the soil around the tree and also to water it more than the other two trees. The more attention we gave this tree, the more it withered and dried up. Meanwhile I continued to pray against any planting that was not planted by my Father to be pulled up by the roots. All the leaves fell from this tree until it was bare. Meanwhile the other two trees were green and healthy. The tree started to twist as it dried up.

One afternoon our landlord called me and told me that he wanted to come and show his uncle the house. They arrived at about two in the afternoon. The "uncle" that he brought was a young man who was dressed in a long white gown. They quickly walked to the garden and I followed them. Then the landlord went to the dry tree and said, "This is where I planted it!" The "uncle" who I later learnt was a witchdoctor said with frustration, "But it is dead!" It was at this point that they realised that I had heard their conversation. They quickly excused themselves and left our compound. I later learned that landlords would plant a particular tree in the yard that would act as a "monitoring spirit." This tree would be used to control and manipulate the tenants. The landlord would know what is going on with his tenants and manipulate the tenants so that any time they increased the rent, the tenant would be in agreement. Our prayers caused the tree to dry up and die although we were not specifically targeting the particular tree. We were not even aware that such a tree was in our garden. This is to let us know that the Spirit that indwells us is far greater and stronger than any evil spirit that Satan can send against us. We also do not always have to know exactly what the witchdoctor has done, in order for us to be set free. God has given us the authority to overcome all the power of the enemy! – Luke 10:19

In East Africa one of the things among many things that witchdoctors do is to plant black magic bottles in the compound of unsuspecting victims. These bottles often contain something representing the DNA of the person targeted – hair, nails, cloth, teeth, bones etc. Once a bottle has been planted in the compound, strife leading to separation of a couple may occur. Other occurrences may be confusion, stagnation, incurable sicknesses, accidents, death, sudden poverty, lack, or general failure in everything that a person does.

The important thing to remember about black witchcraft is that it is a deliberate attempt to harm an unsuspecting person. The power of black magic is often demonstrated through spoken curses. These are words intended to invoke a supernatural power (an evil spirit) to inflict harm or punishment on a victim. The Bible tells us that in the tongue, is the power of life and death (Proverbs 18:21). The tongue of a witchdoctor can produce death if it is not countered by the redemption that Jesus Christ bought for us through His death on the cross of Calvary!

## PRAYER

Heavenly Father, I thank you that you have given us authority to trample on snakes and scorpions and to overcome all the power of the enemy! Through the death of Jesus Christ we have power to overcome the powers of darkness that comes from black witchcraft. Thank you for teaching me how black witchcraft works. Your Word tells us not to be unaware of the devil's schemes. I also thank you that He who is in me (The Holy Spirit), is greater than he who is in the world (The devil). I take authority as a servant of the Living God and break every power of black witchcraft that has been used against me in the name of Jesus Christ. I cancel all **divination, sorcery, spells, hexes, spoken curses, incantations and charms** being used against me in the name of Jesus Christ! I pull down all the altars from which black witchcraft is being used against me! I command all spirits of black witchcraft to leave me now in the name of Jesus Christ! Breathe out deeply several times. You may feel like yawning or coughing. You may even feel sensations in your hands and feet. I am set free in the mighty name of Jesus Christ! And he who the Son sets free is free indeed!

Chapter Five

# Witchcraft and Blood Covenants

A covenant is any relationship that is entered into by two parties. If you have entered into a contract, then you have entered into a covenant. If you are married, then you have entered into a covenant. Two people come together and swear by an oath that they will abide by certain stipulations. If one party fails, then there will be due punishment. The covenant I have just talked about involves two equal parties. There are however covenants that involve two unequal parties. This is the kind of covenant that is made between a person and a deity (Satan or God).

God made a covenant with Abram. It was a covenant to bless him so that his descendants would be as numerous as the stars in the sky, and also to give him the land of Canaan. Abram asked God how he could know that he was going to take possession of the land. Let us see how God made this covenant. *"So the Lord said to him, 'Bring me a heifer, a goat and a ram, each three years old, along with a dove and a young pigeon. Abram brought all these to him, cut them in two and arranged the halves opposite each other…when the sun had set and darkness had fallen, a smoking firepot with a blazing torch appeared and passed between the pieces. On that day the Lord* made a covenant with Abram and said, 'To your descendants I give this land, from the river of Egypt to the great river, the Euphrates..."* – Genesis 15:9-10,17-18.

According to this covenant that God made with Abram, animals were brought, blood was shed, and a promise was made (something was spoken). In the Old Testament, the sacrificing of animals was required for a covenant to be made. However, in the book of Jeremiah we see the advent of a new covenant.

Finally God told them in Jeremiah 31:31 *"**Behold the days are coming, declares the Lord, when I will make a new covenant with the house of Israel and the house of Judah...**"* Jesus Christ was the fulfilment of this new covenant. Before Jesus went back to heaven He told His disciples at the Lord's supper, *"**This cup is the new covenant in my blood...whenever you drink this cup you proclaim the Lord's death...**"* – 1 Corinthians 11:25. The new covenant was ushered in by the death of Jesus Christ through the shedding of his blood. This was done once and for all. The new covenant is salvation that brings forgiveness, freedom, health, and prosperity through the blood of Jesus Christ. We enter into a covenant with God when we accept His son and it is sealed through the blood of Jesus Christ. The word covenant in the Hebrew language, means "cut" and the evidence of the cut was blood. The blood- sacrifice sealed the covenant.

Satan after having seen how God made covenants, decided to copy Him. Satan knows that covenants are agreements, they are binding, and that they are sealed through the shedding of blood and the speaking of words. When a person goes to see a witchdoctor, and the witch doctor slaughters an animal, they get into a binding agreement that has been sealed through the shedding of blood. Most people who go to see witchdoctors often say that he or she made some incantations, which they do not remember. The incantations are often the promises that are made to demonic powers. These spoken words have power to change circumstances. The covenant made with Satan through the witchdoctor will stand until it is broken through the power of Jesus Christ. When God made a covenant with Noah after the Flood, He told him, *"I now establish my covenant with you and with your descendants after you."* – Genesis 9:9. Covenants are never made only with the person making it but also with the descendants. When God made a covenant with Abram, he told him *"To your descendants I give this land…"* – Genesis 15:8. Satan is not only after the life of the person who makes a covenant with witchdoctors, but also after their descendants. A person's descendants are affected up to the third and fourth generation when they worship another god by going to see a witchdoctor (Exodus 20:5). Involvement in witchcraft with blood covenants is the most effective way of Satan binding many generations at once. It is also for this reason that God detests witchcraft!

In 2 Kings 3:24-27, we see the power of a blood covenant. The Israelites and the Moabites were at war and the Israelites were much stronger than them. *"When the Moabites came to the camp of Israel, the Israelites rose up and fought them until they fled. And the Israelites invaded the land and slaughtered the Moabites… When the king of Moab saw that the battle had gone against him, he took with him seven hundred swordsmen to break through to the king of Edom, but they failed."* –verse 24-26. It is often when people have tried to solve their own problem and failed, that they will seek the services of a higher power. This is as true with Christians, as it is also true with non-Christians. So it is only after the Moabite king had tried to defeat Israelite through physical means and failed, that he resorted to spiritual means. Listen to what he did. *"Then he took his firstborn son, who was to succeed him as king, and offered him as a sacrifice on the city wall."* – verse 27. For the king, desperate times called for desperate measures! He killed his own first-born son thus making a blood covenant with the powers of darkness. The agreement was that he offers his son in exchange for demonic help to defeat Israel. According to people who are in the occult, the sacrifice of the first-born son is the highest and most powerful covenant that one can make with Satan! What was the result of this blood covenant that the king of Moab made? *"...The fury against Israel was great..."* All of a sudden the tide turned and the Moabites received demonic strength! How could this be? How could the Moabites defeat the children of Almighty God? What was the final outcome of this added strength against the Israelites? *"...They withdrew and returned to their own land."* What a story! Israel who had earlier thoroughly defeated the Moabites, were forced to withdraw and return to their own land. Why did the Moabites win? It was because they made the highest sacrifice to demonic powers. Israel could not make a sacrifice that was greater than the Moabites because God did not allow them to sacrifice human beings. *"Let no one be found among you, who sacrifices his son or daughter..."* – Deuteronomy 18: 10. The Israelites had no choice but to retreat.

God sacrificed His first-born Son, the highest sacrifice that will cancel and nullify any demonic power that can ever come against us through witchcraft! Hallelujah! Jesus Christ is the eternal sacrifice that God made to defeat the kingdom of darkness! *"They overcame him by the blood of the Lamb..."* – Revelation 12:11.

Incisions on the body are blood covenants with the demonic world. When a witchdoctor cuts a person's body and rubs in the black powder he is making a covenant on your behalf and on your descendants behalf, with the kingdom of darkness. Satan wants blood because *"The life of every creature is its blood"* – Leviticus 17:14. I have counselled many young people who cut themselves when they are depressed. When I was working as a counsellor in a Christian school in west Africa, a young European man was brought to me who had cut marks the length of his whole arm! At the time I did not understand why he felt the urge to cut himself. He said that a voice would tell him to cut himself. In retrospect I can now see how Satan wanted to bind him to the demonic world through these blood covenants.

In the account of the competition between the prophet Elijah and the prophets of Baal we again see this principle of Satan wanting blood. When the prophets of Baal had called on him for hours yet fire did not come down to burn their sacrifice, they resorted to the blood covenant. *"So they shouted louder and slashed themselves with swords and spears, as was their custom, until their blood flowed"* – 1 King 18:28.

We find the final example in the book of Mark chapter 5 when Jesus confronts a demon- possessed man who lived in the tombs. We are told that, *"Night and day among the tombs and in the hills he would cry out and cut himself with stones"* – Mark 5:5. Each time this man cut himself he bound himself deeper with the demonic world through his blood.

## PRAYER

Heavenly Father, I thank You for teaching me in this chapter about blood covenants. Please forgive me for any blood covenants that I have made or have been made on my behalf by my ancestors. I renounce and denounce any blood covenant that has ever been made on my behalf. I nullify and break the yokes of slavery, fetters, chains or shackles that bind me because of blood covenants in the name of Jesus Christ! Lord Jesus You are my Advocate. Please cleanse my sins with Your blood. Heavenly Father, silence the Accuser on my behalf and declare me clean. I command all evil spirits that are clinging to me because of blood covenants to leave me in the name of Jesus Christ! Come out of every part of my body by the blood of Jesus! Come out of every incision in the name of Jesus Christ!

Chapter Six

# Areas touched by Witchcraft

There is one reason for which people solicit the services of witchdoctors – Jealousy. Jealousy will never be an issue in the life of a person who truly understands why God created them. A person pursuing his or her purpose has no time to be jealous of anyone! They understand that they are in a race where they should be constantly trying to beat their own record – To be the best version of themselves! However, a jealous person's focus is on their neighbour's achievement. They are more worried about their neighbour's record rather than their own. If their neighbour builds a three-bedroom house then they will build a four-bedroom house even if they have to borrow the money to do it! They are never content with what they have as long as their neighbour has something which they feel is better than theirs. Happy and contented people are those whose goal is to beat their own record in any achievement. There are however people who will not rejoice over their 95% in mathematics if their classmate gets 98%!

People who compete with their neighbours are the most likely people to go and see a witchdoctor so that their neighbour can fail in a particular area. Once a person goes to see a witchdoctor to "fight" a neighbour, there are many areas that can be touched by the witchcraft spell. Let us look at some of the areas that the spell can touch.

## 1) FINANCES

In many places in Africa, polygamy is synonymous with witchcraft. When the second wife is brought into the home, the first wife and her children, are often neglected. After a period of time the first wife will often be advised by a friend to go and see a witchdoctor to "fix" the second wife and her children.

A young lady came to see me for counsel. She told me that every time she got a job, it would not last six months. Whenever she got a job it started very well. Her immediate supervisor was often very please with her. Then all of a sudden he or she would turn against her and criticize her performance. Because of constantly being let go of from her places of work, she was always in dire financial need. She was reduced to a life of borrowing money from her friends and relatives and not being able to pay back. Apparently she was not the only member of her family who suffered this predicament. She told me that what she was going through was a pattern that she had seen with her siblings as well. I was curious to find out why this pattern was following her and her siblings. When I asked her to tell me a little bit about her family background she told me that her mother was the second wife in a polygamous family. Her mother's older sister had told her that the first wife was rumoured to have gone to a witchdoctor to curse the second wife and her children. She was also rumoured to have said that the children of the second wife would "beg for bread" for the rest of their lives. "It is true that my siblings and I are always begging! None of us is stable financially. My stepmother died last year. We don't know what to do." Despite this lady being a Christian and a leader in her church, the same predicament that befell her siblings who were not believers, also befell her. That was her greatest frustration. She has prayed faithfully for a "breakthrough" to no avail!

Common trends where a person's finances are being manipulated through witchcraft are:

- Any time one starts a business it goes on very well for a while then comes crashing down, and this happens over and over again!
- Despite one having worked hard for many years, there is nothing to show for it. No property owned, and no savings.
- Living from hand to mouth.
- Constantly losing things and being stolen from.

## 2) HEALTH

There is nothing more personal than a person's health. Pain or discomfort in a person's body is something that clings to them day and night. One visit to a hospital ward is all one needs to understand this principle. Nobody can help you carry your sickness. It is possible to help a friend financially. However when it comes to one's health, each carries their own load. Galatians 6:5 put it very well. **"For each one should carry his own load."** It is easy to see therefore, how witchcraft touching a person's health is one of the worst loads to carry! Sudden and unexplained persistent sickness on a person who has otherwise enjoyed perfect health, is always suspect!

Francis (not his real name), according to his mother, was a perfectly normal child. Other than occasional colds and coughs, he had never suffered any major ailment. However at the age of thirteen and when he was about to sit for a major exam that if he passed would move him from primary school to high school, his face broke out with huge pimples. Francis' mother was not alarmed because she assumed that since he was entering adolescence, the pimples were as a result of the hormonal changes that all young men his age go through. The pimples became sceptic and she was forced to take him to see a dermatologist. One month of using the medical cream that he was given made no difference to his condition. In fact his condition got worse! As Francis scratched the now itching pimples, they broke out into bleeding wounds on his face. Monthly visits to different dermatologists bore no good results for Francis. A biopsy on one of the pimples was done to rule out cancer. The results came out negative. Francis could not sit for his exams because he could not concentrate on his studies. Despair set in as doctor after doctor could not find the cause of Francis' condition. By the time his mother came to see me during a teaching mission to the church she attended, Francis was suicidal and could not be left alone.

I asked his mother when exactly this condition started and what was going on in Francis' life during that period. She told me that she remembered that Francis went to visit a friend over a weekend and when he came back, he started complaining about having headaches. As the same time the pimples also appeared. The headaches ended after taking pain- killers but the pimples became more and more until they covered his whole face. The most significant thing she told me was the fact that Francis' friend's neighbours suspected his friend's mother of practising witchcraft! Francis was an "A" student while his friend struggled with school. After Francis dropped out of school, his mother told me, his friend went on and did his exams and passed very well! "I have prayed and fasted for my son's healing but he has just continued to get worse," Francis' mother told me.

Common trends where a person's health is manipulated through witchcraft:

- Suffering from, persistent recurring sicknesses, diseases, and ailments, of which doctors cannot find the root cause.
- Too many relatives dying from incurable diseases one after another, both Christians and non-Christians!
- When a person falls sick every time they are about to do something very important, for their advancement.

## 3) MARRIAGES

I still remember my son coming home from school when he was only ten years old and telling me that he had a science project that he wanted me to help him with. We discussed together what his project should be and he told me that he wanted to create a "live volcano." I did not want to discourage him but I honestly did not think that he would be able to create a live volcano. After he explained to me what he wanted to do I began to "see" the live volcano with eyes of faith! Lantei took newspapers and tore them into small pieces. Then he soaked them in water and mixed it with glue. While this mixture was still wet, we moulded it into a mountain and created a hole in the middle of it. We waited for it to dry completely and there was our volcano. "So how are we going to make it 'live'"? My son told me that we needed to get some bi-carbonate of soda, and pour it in the hole that we had created. After we did that, he said that the final step was going to be done on the day of the project exhibition. He was going to pour vinegar into the hole with bi-carbonate of soda. He painted the outside of the volcano and the surrounding areas. I was just as excited as him on the day when we took the project to school. Parents walked in with their children as they proudly carried their projects into the class-room. Lantei proudly set his project on the table. When the time came for him to show his project, my son took the vinegar that we had brought and poured it into the hole in the middle of the volcano. The mixture of the bi-carbonate of soda and vinegar started to bubble out of the volcano the same way that a real live volcano would pour out lava. The class exploded into clapping and cheering! Both parents and students were transfixed as the "live volcano" spewed out "lava" to shouts of "Wow!" I had never seen my son that happy in his life!

Marriage was the first project that God made. He created a man and woman and brought them together. ***"Then the Lord God made*** *a woman from the rib he had taken out of the man, and he brought her to the man."* – Genesis 2:22. I can only imagine how happy God was when Adam saw Eve, and with utter amazement said ***"This is now bone of my bones and flesh of my flesh; she shall be called woman, for she was taken out of man."*** – verse 23. This was God's "live volcano!" What was the purpose of God's project? We see it in the following verse ***"For this reason a man will leave his father and mother and be united to his wife, and they will become one flesh"*** – verse 24. When Jesus quoted this verse in Mark 10:9 He added a line ***"Therefore what God has joined together, let no one separate."*** We need to understand that when it comes to witchcraft against a marriage, Satan's ultimate goal is to separate what God has joined together!

Yvonne, (not her real name), was referred to me by a close friend. My friend told me that Yvonne had told her that a woman at her place of work was using witchcraft to control and manipulate her husband! I asked Yvonne to tell me why she was convinced that her colleague had used witchcraft against her marriage. I listened intently as Yvonne, with tears in her eyes, recounted how theirs had been a very happy and fulfilling marriage. Her husband and their two children attended a church where her husband was in the leadership. All was going well until her husband started going for "work trips" on weekends. Of course that meant that he would not go to church with the family. He once told her that a Christian friend at his office had invited him for a men's only retreat. He left on a Friday and came back late on Sunday. When she asked him how the retreat was, he was vague and non-committal. When Yvonne went to work on Monday, a friend told her that she had seen her husband with their colleague, Janet, at a golf club on Saturday. Yvonne asked her husband about this and he denied it and accused her of distrust and listening to rumours! Her husband's attitude towards her began to change immediately. He stopped going to church, prompting the pastor to visit their home. That did not change anything as Yvonne's husband started to disappear on Friday evenings and reappear on Sunday evening. Yvonne's colleague at work confided in her that Janet was known to visit witchdoctors and that she had probably used a love portion to get her husband. Yvonne refused to believe it. Her husband was a believer and she was praying for him. The next time that Yvonne brought up the topic of her husband's infidelity, he became violent and physically abusive for the first time since they got married. The next day he packed his clothes and left!

It was two months after Yvonne's husband left that a friend of hers recommended that she come to see me. As Yvonne had been recounting to me the story of her marriage break-up, I kept praying and asking God to reveal to us whether it was witchcraft that had broken her marriage. I was able by the grace of God to see one of the signs.

Common trends when witchcraft has been used to manipulate and control marriages:

- A sudden change in the behaviour of one spouse towards the other. One begins to display uncharacteristic tenancies – anger, violence, no desire for intimacy, finding fault unnecessarily, and avoiding the company of their spouse by spending less and less time at home.
- Not finding their spouse attractive anymore. A husband or wife will start criticizing the appearance of their spouse. They will start to notice and be bothered by things that they were not bothered by before.
- Claiming that their husband or wife is emitting a bad smell! A lady once told me that her husband claimed that every time he came near her, he would smell something bad.
- Obsession with the person who has used the witchcraft "love portion" to attract the man or woman. I once heard on television, the testimony of a man who had used a love portion to get a woman to be attracted to him. He said that he later felt tormented and oppressed, as the lady wanted to be with him, in the same room all the time. She did not

want to let him out of her sight. If he went to the bathroom, she would wait for him outside the door!
- Members of the same family not getting married.
- All siblings getting children out of wedlock before they get married
- Marriages not lasting in a particular family line (Separation and divorce).

## 4) THE MIND

Every action begins as a thought. A person who controls a person's mind, controls their actions as well. It is therefore very easy to see how a witchdoctor who wants to control a person will endeavour to control their mind. The mind is the seat of the emotions. A person will get angry because they have believed or interpreted something in their mind – as disrespect, demeaning, or an attack on their person. If you want to change a person, then change his mind. In Daniel chapter four we read about the punishment of king Nebuchadnezzar from God, when he boasted about his greatness. In Daniel 4: 30, listen to how this foolish king boasted. *"He said, 'Is not this the great Babylon I have built as the royal residence, by my mighty power and for the glory of my majesty?'"* God's judgment was swift! *"The words were still on his lips when a voice came from heaven, 'This is what is decreed for you king Nebuchadnezzar: Your royal authority has been taken from you. You will be driven away from people and will live with the wild animals; you will eat grass like cattle..."* - Daniel 4:31-32. Human beings cannot eat grass and live with wild animals. To act like an animal, God did not need to change king Nebuchadnezzar's body into that of an animal. All God needed to do was to make the king think like an animal. So what did God do? *"Let his mind be changed from that of a man and let him be given the mind of an animal..."* –Daniel 4:16. If you read the whole of chapter 4 you will see how the king started to think like an animal. He went to live with the wild animals and began to eat grass.

About two years ago I saw on Kenyan television, the story of a witchdoctor that could make people eat grass, like an animal! Whenever somebody went to this witchdoctor to tell him that he had been stolen from, he made a spell that caused whoever the thief was to start eating grass! From the story of king Nebuchadnezzar we can see that what the witchdoctor did was to make the thief think that he was an animal. We are who our minds believe that we are! Witchdoctors are able to use demonic power to interfere with the minds of human beings.

Recently I was teaching at a seminar and during the time when we allow people to give testimonies, a lady recounted how her son who was doing engineering in university once came from university to visit his parents and went to visit a neighbour. When he came back he started to act differently. He looked confused and started to say things that did not make sense. The next day he went back to college only to be brought back by his friends who said that he was shouting and talking incoherently. A visit to the doctor revealed that he tested negative for every test done on him. This young man, eventually had to be sedated at all times because he became violent and one time left the house without anybody's knowledge and was found two days later, roaming the streets with only his underwear. What could have happened to this intelligent engineer? Something had messed up with his mind. After prayer and the breaking of a witchcraft spell, the young man "got his mind back" and is back in university today.

Common trends when witchcraft has been used to control the mind:

- A sudden change in behaviour accompanied by irrational thinking. A person begins to believe things that are not true, about themselves and other people, and act on those beliefs – thinking that someone out there wants to kill them; thinking that they are emitting a bad smell; thinking that people are saying negative things about them.

- Sudden bouts of confusion whenever one is about to engage in something very important, for example sitting for a major exam or going for an interview.
- Suddenly unable to understand simple things that they were hitherto able to understand.
- Sudden desire to want to be alone and isolated, because of the belief that people hate them.

## 5) DREAMS

God created sleep so that we can rest our bodies after a hard day's work. Sleep therefore is a gift from God. After a good night's rest most people will wake up refreshed and ready to tackle the next day's work. However there are people who are tormented and oppressed through insomnia. Insomnia is the inability to fall asleep. Whenever I travel to a country with a different time zone, I struggle with insomnia when I go back to my home country. I remember when we lived in London and my husband and I would travel to California for two weeks. The difference in time between London and California is roughly eight hours. Whenever we would come back to London, I would lay awake the whole night and fall asleep towards morning. I can still remember how frustrated and tormented I felt when I would stay awake the whole night. This would go on for about five days then I would settle down to my regular sleep schedule. I cannot even imagine what people go through who struggle with insomnia as a regular life style!

In Psalm 127:2 God says, *"...For he grants sleep to those he loves."* We see through this verse, that sleep is one way that God shows us love. King David in Psalm 4:8 says, *"I will lie down and sleep in peace, for you alone, O Lord make me dwell in safety."* There are people who lie down and sleep. However there are those who lie down and **sleep in peace.** If Satan wants to harass us then he will make sure that we do not sleep in peace. One of the ways that our peaceful sleep can be disturbed is through tormenting dreams (nightmares). We have said that witchcraft is simply evil spirits on assignment. Evil spirits on assignment from witchdoctors can disturb our sleep through frightening and tormenting dreams. Whereas we are supposed to wake up refreshed after sleeping at night, there are people who dread going to sleep because of nightmares and demonic experiences that they go through at night. In Psalm 91:3-6 God promises to save us from *"The fowler's snare and from the deadly pestilence. He will cover you with his feathers and under his wings you will find refuge…You will not fear the terror of night,…Nor the pestilence that stalks in the darkness…"*. What is the terror of night? What about the pestilence that stalks in the darkness?

Many people have recounted to me how they are terrified of the night because of the demonic attacks that they experience. They tell of being chocked as they sleep on their bed or feeling like there is an unseen presence in their room. People speak of seeing shadows moving in their rooms at night. The verses we have read above tell us that these are not figments of people's imagination. For these tormented individuals, sleep which is a gift from God and which should bring rest and refreshment become something that they dread. Witchdoctors are able to torment people through the "Terror of night" and "The pestilence that stalks in the darkness." There are also those that are tormented by "spirit wives"(succubus) and "spirit husbands" (incubus). According to the dictionary, succubus is a female demon believed to have sexual intercourse with sleeping men, while incubus sleeps with sleeping women. The first time I ever heard of spirit husband was in West Africa when one of the young girls in my Sunday school class told me that there was a spirit that used to come and sleep with her at night. The phenomenon was as strange as telling me that she had given birth to a cat! I really found it hard to believe what she was telling me until three or four other women corroborated her claim. It can only be sheer torment for a person to experience a spirit having sex with them. At the end of the day, all these night terrors are to keep a person from having a restful sleep so that they cannot function at their optimum level during the day. This leads to feeling sleepy during the day, which can cause a person not to think clearly and can even cause them to eventually lose their job. So if a witchdoctor wants to torment a person then they will send evil spirits on assignment to keep the person from sleeping through wicked dreams.

Common trends when witchcraft is being used to manipulate dreams:

- Always dreaming about speaking with people who have already died.
- Always dreaming of being chased by snakes or always seeing lots of snakes crawling all over the place.
- Dreaming of someone sitting on their chest and strangling them.
- Always dreaming of being chased by black dogs.
- Miscarriage after dreaming of someone squeezing the stomach or snatching a baby from you. I met a lady who had miscarried six times and each time it was after she had had a similar dream.
- Always losing things in dreams.
- Dreaming that you are back in school and not able to do exams.
- Always dreaming that you are back in the home where you grew up.
- Waking up sweating, and with heart palpitations and aware that you had a nightmare but not able to remember what the dream was about.

## 6) EDUCATION

Some of the saddest cases where witchcraft has been used are on education. A brilliant young man who has been an A student since primary school goes to university to study economics. He is very brilliant in class but every time he has to do a test or exam, he fails! The lecturers are baffled. He is very hard- working and an active participant in class. What is going on? He confides in a good friend that whenever he sits down do an exam, he suddenly becomes confused and cannot understand the questions.

Jealousy is very common in polygamous homes. Quite often the first wife will use witchcraft against the children of her rival co-wife. The second wife will also, in retaliation, use witchcraft against the children of the first wife. A Christian woman whose husband married a second wife told me that she was sure that the second wife had cursed her children through witchcraft. Her children were all doing well in school until her husband married a second wife. Then all of a sudden her children started failing their exams and struggling in the area of education. I know a young man who would get straight 'A's in his course work. As soon as he approached the exams his grades would start to go down and eventually get a 'C' in his exam. This puzzled both him and his teachers. I can only imagine the frustration of a bright child who cannot pass their exams.

Another mother also told me that she suspected her mother-in-law who hated her of having cursed her son who was bright but kept repeating classes. Why would anyone want to use witchcraft against the education of somebody else's child? This is because in many Third World countries, success in life is pegged on how well one did in school.

Common trends when witchcraft has been used against a person's education:

- Constantly falling sick during exam time.
- Sudden negative change in the performance of a student who has otherwise been doing very well in school.
- Experiencing panic attacks when one sits down to do an exam. This would be in the case of somebody who before this did not have such a problem.

- Members of the same family never doing well in education, no matter how hard they try.
- Members of the same family dropping out of school in a particular grade.

---

### PRAYER

Heavenly Father, Hosea 4:6 tells us that we perish for lack of knowledge. Thank you for the knowledge that I have gotten from reading this chapter on the different areas of life that can be touched or affected by witchcraft. Please help me know if there is any area in my life that has been touched by witchcraft. Thank you for your Word which tells us, that greater is He who is in us, than he who is in the world. You have given us the power in Luke 10:19 to overcome all the power of the enemy! Thank you that in this book, You will show me how to completely overcome the power of witchcraft. Thank You for the death of Jesus Christ on the cross of Calvary. It is through that death that I appropriate power to overcome witchcraft. I cover my finances, health, marriage, mind, dreams and education with the blood of Jesus Christ. I declare that no weapon formed against me will prevail in Jesus name! I bind all spirits of witchcraft in any of the areas mentioned in Jesus name! All spirits that have been given an assignment against my finances, health, marriages, mind, dreams and education, I cancel your assignments and I bind you in the name of Jesus Christ. Come out of my life! Leave me now in Jesus name! He who the Son sets free is free indeed!

Chapter Seven

# People likely to use Witchcraft

There is always a reason why a person is drawn towards witchcraft. Not everybody is interested in using witchcraft. To my great surprise, there are people who do not believe that witchcraft exists. It is considered as a primitive belief that holds no water. Whether we like it or not, witchcraft is a reality that dwells in our midst. We heard God speaking against women who were involved in witchcraft among the Israelites in Ezekiel chapter 13, and this witchcraft was being used to trap His people. The Bible recognizes the existence of witchcraft and so must every believer. There are those who say that what you do not know cannot harm you. This could not be further from the truth. The truth is that what you do not know is what will harm you. In Hosea 4:6 God warned the Israelites that they were perishing for lack of knowledge. *"My people are destroyed from lack of knowledge. Because you have rejected knowledge, I also reject you as my priests..."* To say that what you do not know cannot harm you is like saying that, if I do not know that there is a lion hiding in a bush ahead of me, it will not harm me!

Let us now look at people who are most likely to be drawn into witchcraft. Witchcraft is basically the desire to control a situation or an outcome.

## STEP MOTHERS

The death of a mother can be very traumatising for a baby or a little child. However death is a reality and many children have had grown the misfortune of growing up without a biological mother. In many cases like this, a widower left with small children has remarried and his new wife has taken over the care of his destitute children. Women who have stepped into this role and taken good care of children borne by somebody else are worthy of praise and great honour! I have met people who have told me that they only learned as adults, that the woman they thought was their biological mother was actually their step- mother. This speaks volumes about the gracious and kind heart of such a woman!

However, the step- mother that I am discussing here is not the step- mother that comes into a home after a mother has passed on, but the woman who comes into the family as a second or third wife while the first wife is still married to her husband. This is called polygamy. In many countries in Africa, there are situations where a man will marry many wives. I recently counselled with a person who told me that their grandfather had six wives and many children! In polygamous families witchcraft is often rampant. Jealousy and competition for the man's attention will often end with the wives going to solicit the services of a witchdoctor so that their husband can favour them and their children. Resources are often scarce since it has to be shared among many people. One of the wives losing child after child, is not uncommon in polygamous homes. One of the wives not being able to get children is often blamed on witchcraft from one of the co-wives. Seeing the children of a co-wife doing well in school often causes jealousy and can attract a desire to curse them through witchcraft. It becomes a survival tactic where the wives in a polygamous family find it prudent to protect themselves and their children. Apart from using witchcraft against each other, the wives in a polygamous home often use witchcraft on their husband through love portions. These are often put in his food, or smeared on his clothes and belongings. It is curious to note that in most polygamous homes, it is the husband who dies first.

## MOTHERS - IN - LAW

Most mothers have a very strong bond with their children. God made it that way for the protection of the baby. From the moment that a child is born their very survival depends on their mother. This relationship often grows from strength to strength as the mother gives of her life to ensure that her child survives all the dangers of being alive in this world. Then a time comes for "leaving and cleaving". ***"For this reason a man will leave his father and mother and be united to his wife, and they will become one flesh."*** – Genesis 2:24. Most mothers-in-law do not want to be left for the wife! In many African cultures this verse has totally been done away with so that it reads, "For this reason a woman will leave her father and mother and be united to her husband's family and be one with them." Some cultures in Kenya require that the son's wife come and live with her mother-in-law who then becomes her superintendent and commander- in-chief! The mother-in-law gladly controls her son, daughter-in-law and grandchildren. In some cases, if her son wants to marry a second wife she will gladly welcome the new "visitor." In cases where she lives in the village while her son works and lives in the city with his wife and children, great animosity and jealousy often develop towards her daughter-in-law. She often sees her daughter-in-law as a stranger who has come and taken her son's affections, attention, and finances from her. Unfortunately it is often at this point that some mothers-in-law will resort to witchcraft to gain back control over their son. It is not uncommon for a man's behaviour towards his wife to suddenly change because of witchcraft from his mother.

A young lady who had only been married for three years told me how every time her mother-in-law (who is know to visit witchdoctors) visits from the village, her husband and her will quarrel the whole time she is there and her visits do not last less than two months. During that same period their two-year old son would have nightmares almost every night and she would have headaches that do not respond to pain-killers.

There are some wonderful mothers-in-law who should really be called "mothers-in-love". They see themselves not as having lost a son, but as having gained a daughter. I met one such daughter who told me that her mother-in-law was her best friend! The Bible tells us of the story of Ruth and her mother-in-law Naomi. There was such great love between them that even after her husband died Ruth chose to stay with her mother-in-law. *"But Ruth replied, 'Don't urge me to leave you or to turn back from you. Where you go I will go, and where you stay I will stay. Your people will be my people and your God my God. Where you die, I will die and there I will be buried. May the Lord deal with me, be it ever so severely, if anything but death separates you and me."* – Ruth 1:16-17. What a testimony of how the relationship between a mother-in-law and her daughter-in-law should be!

## A REJECTED LOVER

Gladwell (not her real name) was engaged to a fine young man according to everybody around her. All the preparations towards the impending wedding were well underway. The two families considered each other as in-laws. Everybody was excited except Gladwell. There were character flaws that she had started to see in her fiancé. She had resigned herself to the fact that she was going to marry Steven (not his real name), until she shared her misgivings concerning her impending wedding and subsequent marriage with a close friend. "Then why are you marrying him?" her friend asked her. "Because it is too late to change my mind!" Gladwell retorted with anger in her voice. "Gladwell, a broken engagement it better and less painful than a broken marriage. Talk to Steven and tell him the truth. Then talk to your parents. Nobody will be happy but at least you will have saved yourself and your future children from a broken marriage," was the advice from Gladwell's friend. Gladwell talked to Steven and told him that she did not have peace about marrying him. She did not tell him about the serious character flaws that concerned her. She gave him back her engagement ring. "For the shame you have caused me, you will regret this decision for the rest of your life! Mark my words!" was all that Steven said, as he battled tears. When Gladwell shared her decision with her parents, her father stood up and left the room. "What is this you are telling us? Do you have no shame? How do you expect us to face the community?" her mother shouted amidst fast-flowing tears.

It was eight years since this incident took place, that Gladwell came to see me. I could see that she was still tormented by that decision that she had made. Steven had gone ahead and married exactly a year after their break-up. However Gladwell had been involved in four relationships, which did not work. "I suspect that Steven did witchcraft on me. After we broke up I started having nightmares. One time I dreamt that I was running out of a church building wearing a wedding dress with all the guests still in church. Many times I dream about Steven but when I wake up, I am not able to remember what the dream was about. Many times when I get into a relationship, I start losing interest in the person as soon as he starts to get serious with our relationship. Sometimes the person just stops communicating with me and stops picking up my calls although we have not quarrelled."

Most deliverance ministers are in agreement that rejection leads to bitterness. While bitterness, is the root, there are other spirits that a person has to also deal with when helping a person overcome bitterness. These spirits are resentment, unforgiveness, anger and retaliation, just to mention a few. Often the spirits of retaliation and anger will drive a rejected person to go and seek the services of a witchdoctor to hit at the person who has rejected them. One would wonder why the witchcraft actually works against the offender? In the story of Gladwell, why did it seem like the witchcraft worked? Wasn't she right in breaking off the engagement because she could see that there were going to be problems in the future?

In Proverbs 26:2 we read, *"…**An undeserved curse does not come to rest.**"* What made Gladwell liable for the curse to rest on her? What made her deserving of the curse? In a later chapter we will understand why the curse rested on Gladwell.

I have met many people who tell me that after they broke off a relationship with a former lover, they cursed them, saying that they will never get married. A distraught mother of a five- year old girl who had never spoken since she was born came to see me. She told me how when she broke up with the father of the girl when she was only three- months old, the baby's father told her that his daughter would never speak as long as he was alive! True to his words, although doctors could not find the cause of her malady, the beautiful girl had never said a word for five years! The chapter on "White Witchcraft" will explain to us why the father's words came to pass.

## LANDLORD

Peter (not his real name) has lived with his family in a dilapidated house for fifteen years. Many times Peter has not been able to come up with his rent on the fifth of the month as his landlord demands.

Although he manages to pay his rent by the fifteenth of the month and never defaulted for the last 15 years, his landlord has made it a sport to call him on the sixth or seventh of every month to harass him and threaten him with eviction. Although Peter's landlord is quick to demand for his money, he has not made a single renovation to the house since Peter and his family moved in. Many times Peter has had to mend things that have broken down because of age. The landlord has never refunded him for the repairs nor acknowledged the fact that his tenant has tried to keep the house in good order. His wife has urged him for them to look for another house where they can live in peace without harassment from the landlord. Peter has always been reluctant to move although he has had no good reason for wanting to continue staying under such a wicked landlord. Twice his wife has found a house where they would end up paying less rent yet the house was in better condition. Both times Peter gave many reasons why they should not move. Why are there situations where a person is not able to move from a house where they are being harassed by the landlord, and where they are getting very poor services? It is not hard to see how a landlord would want to use witchcraft to control their tenant so that they do not move from their house thus losing the regular income from rent. Witchcraft will also cause a tenant to stay in a house where they are not happy with the services yet continue staying there. One of the ways that a landlord may control the tenants is by burying a witchcraft object on the property. There are tenants who have complained of strange occurrences in their house - Strange noises, unexplainable shadows, bad smell in certain rooms, nightmares. A person who experiences these occurrences in their house should pray and ask God if the landlord is using witchcraft to control them. Peter was was not aware that his landlord was using witchcraft on his family until God revealed it to him in a time of prayer. It is worthwhile to analyse your relationship with your landlord. Are there things that do not make sense? Have you lived in a house where you are not satisfied with the services accorded by your landlord and yet you are unable to move? It is time to ask God whether witchcraft is involved.

## OFFICE COLLEAGUES

There is no place where there is more jealousy than between competing businesses and office colleagues. A friend once told me how the personal assistant to her immediate boss really hated her. Other colleagues in the office also remarked how this person hated her and never passed up a opportunity to talk badly about her behind her back. On her birthday, the office threw a surprise party for my friend. She was very alarmed and surprised when it was her nemesis that handed a gift to her with a very broad smile! She hesitatingly took the gift, wondering if that broad smile was genuine. She was grateful for the gift and touched that her colleagues would each donate money for a gift as was the regular practice at the office. When my friend got home she decided to open the gift and see what her colleagues had bought her. As she was unwrapping the gift, it slipped from her hands and fell to the floor. She heard the sound of breaking glass. She was disappointed as she picked up the box. She shook it and could hear the sound of pieces of broken glass. She decided that since it was broken, she should just throw it away without opening it. She felt led to go and throw it in the bin that was outside the house. Her spirit was disturbed and she wondered why that gift broke before she opened it! The next day as she entered the office she noticed how shocked her boss' assistant was to see her! She later learnt that it was her who had offered to buy her the gift. She refused to take money from anybody else saying that she was offering to pay for the gift. She was also the one who wrapped it. My friend told me that she suspected that her boss' personal assistant had probably used witchcraft against her through that gift! She felt like it was God who did not allow her to open the gift as a way of protecting her from harm. Many people have talked of finding witchcraft paraphernalia in their offices. There are people who will try and manipulate their bosses so that they can get a promotion by using demonic powers. Others, through sheer jealousy, will try and get a colleague fired or for them to stay in the same position while others are being promoted. If you find that your boss is never satisfied with your work no matter how well you work, or that you have stayed in the same position for years while people who you once supervised are promoted to be your boss, you may be dealing with witchcraft!

## PRAYER

Heavenly Father, You have not given us a spirit of fear, but of power, love and a sound mind (2 Peter 1:3). Thank you that we are not victims but victors! In Christ we are always on the winning side. Because of this fact, we should not fear witchcraft. You have told us not to be unaware of the devil's schemes (2 Corinthians 2:11). I thank you that He who is in us, is far greater than he who is in the world. You defeated Satan and made a public show of him when Jesus died on the cross of Calvary! Thank you for teaching us about all the people that are likely to use witchcraft against us. I pray for everybody that is using witchcraft on me to turn to you for salvation otherwise they will end in the Lake of Fire! I come against all witchcraft powers that may be working against me from a stepmother, mother-in-law, a rejected lover, my landlord, or at the office. I pull down all the altars from which they are operating against me, and my family, in the name of Jesus Christ! All evil spirits that have been given assignments against my life and the lives of my family members I command you to lose your hold and get out of our lives in the name of Jesus Christ! I cancel your assignments in the powerful and mighty name of Jesus Christ! We are set free in the name of Jesus Christ. Come out in the name of Jesus Christ!

## Chapter Eight

# White Witchcraft

White witchcraft operates on manipulation and control just like black witchcraft. Both black witches and white witches are used to accomplish Satan's mission to steal, kill and destroy. The grave danger with white witches is that they are often unaware that Satan is using them for his dark purposes. In most cases, a white witch does not know that they are practising witchcraft. While a black witch is confined to a mysterious dark room surrounded by witchcraft paraphernalia, white witches wear clean jeans and dresses and move freely among us! Evil spirits work with white witches the same way that they work with black witches. White witches also use the power of the spoken word, only they are often unaware of the impact of their words. They are usually people in authority. In Hebrews 7:7 we are told *"And without doubt the lesser person is blessed by the greater."* By virtue of this verse, if the lesser person is blessed by the greater then it also follows that the lesser can also be cursed by the greater. So people who have authority over us can curse us through the words that they speak over us.

Proverbs 18:21 tell us *"The tongue has the power of life and death, and those who love it will eat its fruit."* The tongue is like a tree that bears fruit. Once you plant a seed and it grows into a tree, it is bound to bear fruit. In James 3:6-8 we are also told, *"The tongue is also

# White Witchcraft

*a fire, a world of evil among the parts of the body...And is itself set on fire by hell...It is a restless evil, full of deadly poison."* There are certain things that these two verses say about our tongues (and subsequently our words) that are worth noting.

- The tongue can create or destroy.
- What comes out of the tongue will bear fruit.
- The tongue is equated to a fire, and fire consumes.
- The tongue is an evil part of the body.
- The tongue is set on fire by hell.
- The tongue is a restless evil.
- The tongue is full of deadly poison.

Anyone who wants to kill and destroy will find a very powerful ally in the tongue! Through white witchcraft let us see how Satan uses the tongue to steal, kill, and destroy.

Evil spirits listen to our words. Once an evil word comes out of our mouth, they set out on assignment to accomplish what it says. This is why Ephesians 4:29 warns us, **"Do not let any unwholesome talk come out of your mouth, but only what is helpful for building others up according to their needs, that it may benefit those who listen."** Words are an effective tool in Satan's hands, that he can use to destroy. James 3:6 tell us that the tongue can corrupt the whole person and set the course of his life on fire. How many people have had their lives corrupted and the course of their life changed negatively because of something that was said to them?

## CONTROL AND MANIPULAION

Since witchcraft is about control and manipulation, any time a person tries to get people to do what they don't want to do, they are acting as a white witch. A classic white witch is a man or woman who controls the family in a domineering way. All family decisions have to pass through them otherwise nothing moves. Their approval is sought for in all matters. Through control and manipulation, they always get their way, and their decision is final. Anyone who does not toe the line is isolated and disregarded in family matters. This person is operating as a white witch. Another form of white witchcraft is also what is called "soulish" prayer. This is the kind of prayer where we ask God to make somebody do something that they are unwilling to do. When a woman prays and asks God to make a man love her, she is acting as a white witch. God will never interfere with a person's free will. No one is duty bound to do what somebody else wants. They should do what the Holy Spirit wants them to do, according to God's purpose for their life. My son should not stop smoking or drinking for my sake. He should do it for the sake of God's plan for his life. From time to time we have all acted like white witches. We have said words that have given evil spirits occasion to change the course of people's lives negatively. Let us look at some authority figures that have been used by Satan as white witches.

## PARENTS

Parents are the people that God chose, through whom every human being comes to this earth. Parents are supposed to protect their children, and provide for their physical and emotional needs. By the time a child leaves his or her parents' home to go and fend for themselves, they should be able to look back and be grateful for all that their parents did for them so that they can be well integrated into the society. A person should be able to say, "It is because my parents believed in me and encouraged me, that I am who I am today."

Many tears have been shed in my office during counselling sessions, from people who recall the hurtful words that their parents said to them as they were growing up. Proverbs 11:9 says *"With their mouths the godless destroy their neighbours, but through knowledge the righteous escape."* We see from this verse that a person can destroy a neighbour just by using words. When we destroy people through our words, we become white witches. We also see from this verse that through knowledge, the righteous escape. Knowledge is power. Knowing what to do when words that destroy have been used on us can help us escape the negative effects of the words. When a person uses negative words concerning our future, we should cancel them in the name of Jesus Christ.

Unfortunately a little child has no way of cancelling or reversing negative words that have come from a parent. We have said that evil spirits wait for negative words so that they can accomplish them. A young lady told me how her father told her, "You will be a prostitute!" This father was upset at what his daughter was wearing. What was the effect of these negative words? Apart from being very hurt, and still remembering what her father told her twenty years earlier, this lady ended up living a very promiscuous lifestyle! A **spirit of immorality** entered this young lady through her father's words. Because of the authority that he had over his daughter, this father ended up cursing her and became a white witch.

Many parents in a moment of disappointment and frustration at what seems to them as their child's laziness and disinterest in education, often tell their children, "You will never make it! You will be a failure in life!" When a parent says these discouraging words to their children, they give opportunity for **evil spirits of failure** to come upon them. It is no wonder that children who have never been encouraged while growing up often end up not doing well in life.

Every child is unique. Psalm 139:16 tells us that before each child was born, a book was written about them. This book probably contains who their parents will be and the career that God has created for them. It is therefore unfair to compare a child with their sibling. It is the duty of parents to help a child find out what their gifting is and to encourage them in that gifting. When a parent asks their child, "Why can't you be like your sister?" or "Why can't you be like your brother?" a spirit of discouragement, jealousy towards the sibling being praised, and low self-esteem may set in. The same way that evil spirits will use the words of a black witch to cause harm is the very same way that evil spirits will use the words of a "white witch".

Another area where a **spirit of rejection** can enter a child at birth is when a disappointed parent says, "I don't know why she is a girl. We have two girls already! We wanted a boy!" Every human being is a spirit that is living in a body. The spirit in the body of the child hears and understands everything that is said about them. The spirit of rejection often releases a spirit of anger. An angry and rebellious teenager may be that way because of the words spoken over them at birth!

Parents need to be very careful about the words that come out of their mouths. I will remind us again of Ephesians 4:29 that says that no unwholesome talk should come out of our mouths, but only words that build children up according to their needs! Be careful lest you become the white witch in your child's life!

## TEACHER

Teaching is one of the most important professions in the world. A parent will hand over their child to teachers for a period of time, and out comes a doctor, engineer, architect, accountant or businessman! From the age of three (for early beginners) up to the age of eighteen, children spend more time with teachers than they do with parents! Teachers have been given the opportunity to mould the children in their classrooms to be upright members of the society, or to damage them for life. There are many teachers who have seen this wonderful opportunity for what it is, and have moulded the children under their influence into successful members of the society. Unfortunately there are also adults today who have turned to a life of crime, or who struggle with depression, or who have never been successful in life because of what their teachers told them when they were young and vulnerable.

A young lady walked into my office looking very timid and insecure. She told me, how she had just been fired from her third job. Her problem? Whenever she made a mistake and her boss reprimanded her, she would be so gripped by fear that she would stop performing well. She suffered from panic attacks whenever she thought that she might make a mistake in a job that her boss asked her to do. She would be confused and her hands would shake uncontrollably. She became a laughing stock in every place where she worked. I was understandably curious to know how this problem started. Her spiritual mapping (history of her background), revealed that she was brought up, by a single mother. She had never met her father and her mother completely refused to tell her who he was. Right from when she joined nursery school, the teachers would pick on her for ridicule. Amanda (not her real name) was very dark-skinned and small bodied. She told me that her Nursery school teacher would call her "mid-night" because of her skin tone. When she would cry, the teacher would tell her to stand up so that the other children can see how a dark person cries. Amanda spent most of her time crying while the rest of the children laughed at her. She told me that God was gracious to her because she was a bright child and would grasp the concepts that they were taught very quickly. When she would do well, the teacher would say, "Being dark is not that bad after all!" Unfortunately for Amanda, her small stature and dark skin caused her to be teased by children and be picked on by teachers all through her education. By the time she graduated from University with an Accounting Degree, Amanda was a timid, fearful and insecure young lady. She could remember the names of all her teachers from nursery school up till university! Amanda said that despite her teachers calling her "blackie," "pigmy," and "dwarf," she still managed by the grace of God to graduate from university. The problem now was that her timidity, fear, low self-esteem and insecurity caused her to move from job to job. Her teachers were the "white witches" in Amanda's life! Unfortunately Satan used her teachers to chart her life negatively. A teacher who prophesies "doom and gloom" over a pupil is responsible for who that child becomes as an adult. To tell a child, "You are very stupid," or "You will never make it in life!" is to sign up in Satan's register as a "White witch." What that teacher is doing, is sending evil spirits on assignment to afflict that child with failure, fear, timidity, low self-esteem and self-hatred.

## HUSBAND

The Bible tells husbands to love their wives just as Christ loved the Church (Ephesians 5:25). Further in verse 28 this same chapter tells husbands to love their wives as their own bodies. Christ gave His life and shed His blood for the Church. That is how men ought to love their wives. Hebrews 7:7 say that the lesser person is blessed by the greater. Christ is greater than the Church and so is able to bless the Church. By the same token, the wife is supposed to be blessed by her husband. Because it is the Word of God, when a husband blesses his wife, God honours it and endorses the blessing! In this same way, husbands are also able to curse their wives! How can a husband curse his wife? He can do it through his words. Proverbs 18:21 says, **"The tongue has the power of life and death, and those who love it will eat its fruit."** It is therefore easy to see how a husband's tongue can be used for white witchcraft. When a husband tells his wife, "Why can't you think?" he sends a spirit of confusion to attack his wife. A husband who boasts to his wife, "There were many women that I could have married! I did not have to marry you!" he releases a spirit of polygamy into his own home. He should not be surprised if he starts lusting after other women. A spirit of strife and disunity can be granted free access into a home where a husband in anger says, "I don't know why I have such a useless family!"

A husband should strive to be a priest of good will and blessing to his wife and not a source of white witchcraft.

### PRAYER

Heavenly Father, I thank you for teaching me about white witchcraft. You have called me to be a blessing to those around me. Forgive me when I have allowed Satan, through my words, to use me as a white witch! I take authority in the name of Jesus Christ and cancel all the negative words that have been spoken over me through white witchcraft. Whatever words are still affecting me negatively from my parents, teachers, or my husband, I cancel them in the powerful name of Jesus Christ! I declare that I am set free today in the name of Jesus! Spirits of **immorality, failure, low self-esteem, rejection, singlehood, stupidity, confusion, death and polygamy,** I command you to leave me now in the name of Jesus Christ! You have no more power over me!

Chapter Nine

# How safe are you?

Speaking comfortingly to Jerusalem in Zechariah 2:5 God told them, "***And I myself will be a wall of fire around it,*** *" declares the Lord, "**and I will be its glory within.***" With God Himself as a wall of fire, what would dare penetrate that protection? The Bible is replete with verses that reassure believers of the protection that they have from evil. Concerning witchcraft being used against us, there is a verse that brings much comfort and confidence "***No weapon forged against you will prevail, and you will refute every tongue that accuses you. This is the heritage of the servants of the Lord, and this is their vindication from me, declares the Lord.***" The heritage of every believer is that, no weapon formed against him or her prospers. Attacks from witches and wizards should fall off believers the same way that water falls off a duck's back! Why then do we see believers afflicted by witchcraft, as I have recounted in previous chapters?

We have seen that witches are simply agents of Satan that he has lured into his dark kingdom to do his dirty work of stealing, killing, and destroying. Their lust for power makes them vulnerable to the deceptions of the devil. When a witch sends a spell or hex against a person, it is not able to affect them unless there is a "door" through which the curse can enter. Proverbs 26:2 tell us, *"Like a fluttering sparrow or a darting swallow, an undeserved curse does not come to rest."* A curse is compared to a bird that is flying around looking for a place to rest. I have always believed that one cannot stop a bird from flying over his or her head. However they can most certainly stop it from laying an egg on their head! Similarly, we cannot stop witches from sending curses against us, but we can stop the curse from afflicting us. This chapter is about how to stop witchcraft from affecting us. My prayer is that the knowledge gleaned from the Word of God will cause us not to be prey to the diabolical schemes and wiles of witchdoctors! The Bible has already warned us that it is lack of knowledge, and the rejecting of it, that will cause us to perish (Hosea 4:6).

Imagine that you are blessed with a lovely living room, donned with a white carpet, and a white Italian leather sofa set. Outside a huge muddy and smelly pig is running around your house. Let us assume that the most horrific thing you can imagine is that dirty pig coming into the house and making everything dirty! How safe is your pristine living room from the pig? Your living room is safe as long as you can keep that pig from entering your house. How would you ensure that? By making sure that the front and back doors of your house are locked.

In the same way, if we do not want to be affected by witchcraft curses then we need to ensure that all the "doors" of our lives are securely locked! It is not enough to declare, as many believers in Christ do, that "I am covered by the blood of Jesus Christ and no weapon forged against me will not prosper!" If when a curse sent against me by a witch finds an open door in my life, it will most certainly affect me. I therefore want us to discuss a particular doorway that can make us liable to being harmed through witchcraft. One of the main aims of this book is to help us close that doorway.

In the book of Numbers chapter 22 we read about an encounter between Israel and a witchdoctor. The Israelites were the people of God in the same way that believers in Jesus Christ are the children of God. The Israelites had just come out of Egypt where they had been slaves for four hundred and thirty years (Exodus 12:40). God had promised them the land of Canaan, but they had to fight the inhabitants to possess it. In Numbers 22 we see the Israelites camped outside Moab after defeating two powerful kings: Og king of Bashan, and Sihon king of the Amorites. Balak the Moabite king was terrified when he saw the Israelites camped on his land, with the intention to attack him. *"Now Balak son of Zippor saw all that Israel had done to the Amorites, and Moab was terrified because there were so many people. Indeed Moab was filled with dread because of the Israelites."* – Numbers 22:2. King Balak knew that it was not humanly possible to defeat the Israelites. Only a supernatural intervention was going to help them defeat the Israelites. Balak knew a witchdoctor who did not live too far away so he decided to summon him to come and help them through supernatural means. So Balak son of Zippor, who was king of Moab at the time, sent messengers to summon Balaam the witchdoctor with this message, *"Now come and put a curse on these people, because they are too powerful for me. Perhaps then I will be able to defeat them and drive them out of my country…"* - Numbers 22:6. In previous chapters we have talked about the different reasons for which a person would want to curse you. Many times it is because they know that in the physical realm they are unable to do anything to you. They therefore carry the battle to the spiritual realm and often employ the services of a witchdoctor. Should we be worried as believers in Jesus Christ when this happens? Let us see what happened when Balaam the witchdoctor was summoned to curse Israel. This is the only incidence in the Bible where God converses with a witchdoctor. Without dwelling too much on that fact, of importance are the principles that we are able to get from this story. *"But God said to Balaam, 'Do not go with them. You must not put a curse on those people, because they are blessed"* – Numbers 22:12. The only reason for which God would not allow Balaam to curse Israel was because they were blessed. How were they blessed? To understand the principle of curses and blessings we need to read the whole chapter of Deuteronomy chapter 28. In verse fourteen the Lord gave the Israelites the condition for being blessed. This is the only reason why a witchdoctor will not be able to curse you. *"If you fully obey the Lord your God and carefully follow all his commands I give you today, the Lord your God will set you high above all the nations on earth. All these blessings will come upon you and accompany you if you obey the Lord your God."* God was telling Balaam the witchdoctor that he could not curse the Israelites because this verse was true of their lives. They were walking in full obedience to God's commands. What were the Israelites obeying? They were walking in obedience to Deuteronomy 28:14 *"Do not turn aside from any of the commands I give you today, to the right or to the left, following other gods and serving them."* In the next verse, God told the Israelites what would happen if they did not walk in obedience to His commands by following other gods. *"...All these curses will come upon you and overtake you."* Balaam would have been able to curse the Israelites if they had been worshiping other gods. That would have been the doorway that the witchdoctor used to curse them. Those who worship other gods automatically come under God's curse. However Balaam testified of Israel saying, *"No misfortune is see in Jacob, no misery is observed in Israel, the Lord their God is with them…There is no sorcery against Israel, no divination against Israel."* – Numbers 23:23. No misfortune, misery, sorcery or divination can be in the life of a person who is blessed by the Lord!

God eventually allowed Balaam to go to king Balak, but when he opened his mouth only blessings for Israel flowed out! Balak was furious and told the witchdoctor, *"...What have you done to me? I brought you to curse my enemies, but you have done nothing but bless them!" Numbers 23:11.* Indeed a witchdoctor cannot curse someone who is under God's blessing. Balaam had earlier told the king, *"How can I curse those whom God has not cursed?"* A person needs to come under God's curse first before a witchdoctor can curse him or her. So how safe are we? Before we convince ourselves that we are safe let us look at another very pertinent principle concerning worshiping other gods. Exodus 20:5 *"You shall not bow down to them or worship them; for I, the Lord your God, am a jealous God, punishing the children for the sin of the fathers to the third and fourth generation of those who hate me."* Here God is saying that we do not have to have worshipped other gods ourselves but that if our forefathers did, then we are also guilty! Lamentations 5:7 say *"Our fathers sinned and are no more and we bear their punishment."* Unfortunately this means that if my forefathers worshipped other gods then I have an "open door" which can allow a witchcraft curse to touch me! What are these things that our forefathers did? We can see them in Deuteronomy 18:10 *"Let no one be found among you who sacrifices his son or daughter in the fire, who practices divination or sorcery, interprets omens, engages in witchcraft, or casts spells, or who consults the dead. Anyone who does these things is detestable to the Lord, ..."* If our great grandparents, grandparents, parents or ourselves have been involved in the things mentioned in the verse above then we have a generational curse, have open doors, and can be cursed by witchdoctors! Satan has a legal right to use a witchdoctor to curse a believer who is under this generational curse, which is released by God and executed by Satan through his agents.

Balaam knew that he could not curse Israel as long as they were not worshiping other gods. He advised king Balak to have their Moabite women tempt the men to sleep with them so that they could influence them to worship the Moabite gods. Once the men start worshiping their gods then they would come under God's curse and then Balaam would be able to curse them! So the Moabite women tempted the Israelite men, made them fall into sexual immorality with them, and then introduced them to pagan worship! ***"While Israel was staying in Shittim, the men began to indulge in sexual immorality with Moabite women, who invited them to the sacrifices to their gods. The people ate and bowed down before these gods. So Israel joined in worshiping the Baal of Poer. And the Lord's anger burned against them."*** – Numbers 25:1-3. Because of this idolatry (worship of other gods), a plague came on the Israelites and 24,000 Israelites died in one day! Once they worshiped Baal, they, were liable to harm. You and I are not safe from harm, and are liable to fall under a witchcraft spell if we, or our forefathers worshiped other gods! However, praise God who teaches His children through His Word, how to protect themselves from the poison sent by the agents of Satan.

---

### PRAYER

Heavenly Father You have told us that we Your children perish for lack of knowledge. Thank You for the knowledge that I have received as I have read this chapter on my safety. I now realise that thinking that I am safe from witchcraft simply because I am a believer in Christ is misplaced. My forefathers worshiped other gods and have made me liable to witchcraft spells. I thank you for the blood of Jesus that is always available to cleanse me. Show me how to close the doors that are open in my life that would allow dirty pigs to enter my clean "living room." Thank you that in the next chapter, You will help me close all the open doors in my life, in Jesus name I pray – Amen!

## Chapter Ten

# Ensuring our Safety

Our safety depends on how securely we close the doors to our "house". In Matthew 12:44, evil spirits call our body their house. How then do we close the doors to our house? The doors to our houses are opened through sin and so they must be closed through turning away from that sin and repenting. Satan is called the Accuser of the brethren who accuses them before God day and night! – Revelation 12:10. To ensure our safety we need to understand the heavenly courtroom. We should understand that Satan brings accusations against believers in the heavenly courtroom. Every defeat in the physical realm comes as a result of having lost one's case in the heavenly courtroom!

In Daniel chapter seven God is represented as the Ancient of Days in the heavenly courtroom, sitting in as the Righteous Judge. Verse nine starts off by Daniel's view of the throne room of God. *"As I looked, thrones were set in place, and the Ancient of Days took his seat…"* What happens after the Judge takes His seat? We are told that *"…Thousands upon thousands attended him, ten thousand times ten thousand stood before him. The court was seated and the books were opened."* This is the court where Satan brings his accusations! What is in the books that are open? We find the answer in the revelation God gave to the apostle John on the Island of Patmos.

Revelation 20:12 *"And I saw the dead, great and small, standing before the throne, and books were opened… The dead were judged according to what they had done as recorded in the books."* It would seem that the things that are done here on earth are recorded in books in heaven!

Then we see somebody else coming into the courtroom. Daniel continues to tell us, *"In my vision at night I looked, and there before me was one like the son of man, coming with the clouds of heaven. He approached the Ancient of Day and was led into his presence. He was given authority, glory and sovereign power; all peoples, nations and men of every language worshiped him. His dominion is an everlasting dominion that will not pass away, and his kingdom is one that will never be destroyed."* – Daniel 7:13. One does not have to think very hard to know that this passage is talking about Jesus Christ! Jesus Himself testified about this event in Mark 14:62 when He was before the Sanhedrin and the high priest asked him whether He was the Christ, the Son of the blessed One. His response was *"I am, and you will see the Son of Man sitting at the right hand of the Mighty One and coming on the clouds of heaven."* So why is Jesus in the heavenly courtroom? 1 John 2:1 gives away why He is there *"My little children, these things write I unto you, that ye sin not. And if any man sin, we have an advocate with the Father, Jesus Christ the righteous (KJV)."* Praise the Lord! When we are accused in the courtroom and found guilty, our Advocate rises up in our defence! All we have to do is plead guilty and repent. 1 John 1:9 say that if we confess our sins God is faithful and just, and will forgive our sins and cleanse us from all unrighteousness through the blood of Jesus!

What are some of the accusations that Satan brings? Here is an example. "Your son here is guilty of worshiping other gods. His great grandfather was a 'rain maker' and keeper of the village shrine. Your

Word says that the third and fourth generations are also guilty of this sin although they are believers in Jesus Christ. I have the legal right to attack him through his neighbour who is using witchcraft on him. He has an open door!" How does God deal with this accusation? He will first look to see whether the accused person is in the courtroom. Unfortunately many believers do not know that there is a courtroom where they are required to appear. God the Righteous Judge, often with much pain, has to give the legal right to Satan. While Satan is in the courtroom accusing believers, they are often in the battlefield fighting a battle that they have already lost in the courtroom! This is why many well-meaning believers are very prayerful but see not results to their prayers!

Believers in Jesus Christ need to go to the courtroom where their Advocate is ready to plead their case. Believers always win in the courtroom because Jesus' blood will wash any and every sin that a believer confesses. The heavenly courtroom is not a good place for Satan. When a believer appears in the court Satan always loses because the Righteous Judge is our Father and the Advocate is our Saviour!

When we come to the courtroom we must accept that we are guilty as charged and repent, asking God for mercy. We repent for our sins and the iniquities of our forefathers (Sample prayer is found in Daniel 9:16-19). After that we need to call upon our Advocate to cleanse our sin with His blood. Isaiah 1:18 says, *"...Though your sins are like scarlet, they shall be as white as snow; though they are red as crimson, they shall be as wool."* Once we have brought our sins of idolatry to Jesus for cleansing, we can then ask the Righteous judge for a verdict of "Not Guilty" which He always grants. It is after this that we can, through a declaration, break our generational curses as follows:

**And now as a servant of the Living God, I take authority and break every curse over my life from the fourth, third, second and**

first generation. I renounce, denounce, and disconnect myself from the shrines, satanic altars, dedications, spoken curses, broken promises and vow, satanic covenants and oaths that connected me to evil and dark satanic forces! I declare that my mind, emotions, will and body are set free from the control and manipulation of witches and wizards! I am set free in the name of Jesus Christ!

Once, we have been acquitted by the heavenly courtroom we have closed the door and no witchdoctor, can touch our life with curses and hexes. Our safety is assured!

## PRAYER

Heavenly Father, how reassuring it is to know that in Jesus Christ we are safe from the schemes and wiles of witchcraft. Thank You our Righteous Judge for providing a way out of our guilt through the finished work of the cross of Calvary! Although our forefathers opened doors into our lives by worshiping other gods, through the cleansing blood of Jesus Christ we are rendered "Not Guilty!" We can walk in perfect freedom and with no fear because of the way that has been opened into the courtroom. Thank you for Your Word, which says in Hebrews 4:16, *"Let us then approach the throne of grace with confidence, so that we may receive mercy and grace to help us in our time of need."* With the authority that I have been given in Luke 10:19, I command every spirit of **fear, witchcraft, sorcery, divination, astrology, spells, hexes, incantations and spoken curses** to leave me now in the name of Jesus Christ! I seal every doorway as I cover myself with the blood of Jesus Christ! You no longer have any power over me! I am set free in the name of Jesus Christ and he who the Son sets free is free indeed!

## PRAYER FOR SALVATION

The only guaranteed protection that we have against witchcraft is the blood of Jesus Christ shed for us on the cross of Calvary! By making a decision to give our lives to Jesus and make Him Lord of our lives, He becomes our refuge and protector. Acts 4:12 tell us, *"Salvation is found in no one else, for there is no other name under heaven given to men by which we must be saved."* You can make a decision right now to make Jesus Lord of your life. If you are ready to do that, Just say these simple words and mean them from the bottom of your heart . . .

> *"O Lord God, I believe in Jesus Christ the Son of the Living God. I believe He died for me and You raised Him from the dead. Right now I confess with my mouth, Jesus Christ is Lord of my life. I ask you to forgive my sins and to make me Your child. Write my name in the Book of Life! From this day, I thank you Lord for saving my soul. I have eternal life now - In the name of the Lord Jesus Christ. Thank you Lord! I am a child of God from this day forward – Amen! Praise the Lord!"*

If you have prayed this prayer sincerely, you are now born again into the family of God! Find a Bible- believing church and tell the pastor of the decision that you have made. Join a Bible- study group where you can fellowship with other believers so that you can grow. You are now like a new- born baby who needs the milk of the Word. When one sinner gives their life to Jesus Christ, all the angels in heaven rejoice! Welcome into the family of God!

# About the Author

Pastor Nellie is a Kenyan who has been a Christian for over forty years. She is the CEO and Founder of Breaking Barriers International (BBI), a non-profit organization who mission is to equip believers in Jesus Christ to live victoriously and fulfil their purpose in the world. She has adhered to this mission through her teachings on spiritual warfare and deliverance. Her deep revelation of the Word of God is taught, with clarity and simplicity. Besides being an author of eight books, she is also a conference speaker, preacher of the Word of God, and workshop leader. Pastor Nellie has been used by God to teach and train believers in the area of her calling in Africa, the United States of America, the United Kingdom, Eastern Europe, India, and Russia.

As a happily married woman to Dan Ole Shani, she has three grown children and two grandchildren. Pastor Nellie Shani draws much of her knowledge and experience from having lived with her family in six different countries on three continents.

# Other Books by Author

**STAND YOUR GROUND**

Many Christians live a life of defeat, harassed and bombarded by their arch enemy, Satan. They have not yet fully grasped that when Jesus Christ died on the cross, he completely and utterly defeated Satan!

He took back the authority Satan used to deceive Adam and Eve, handing it to the Church. However, our strength is of no use if we don't know we possess it!

This is the tragedy of our Lack of Knowledge.

## Other Books by Author

### BREAKING INVISIBLE BARRIERS

Many Christians today are living a life of constant struggle and failure no matter what they do to try and improve their lot in life. They are fighting something they do not understand.

This book explores these invisible barriers and how to break them by the Power of the Cross.

### HOPE FOR THE CHILDLESS

God designed that every womb He has created be fruitful. Why then do we have people who cannot have children?

This book answers this question and shares the experiences of women who were not able to conceive or carry babies to full term, but today are mothers by the grace of God.

## STEP INTO SUPERNATURAL POWER

Although the Holy Spirit is present and busy in the whole Bible, He is often relegated to the New Testament and more specifically, to the Book of Acts after the Day of Pentecost. What was the Holy Spirit's role in the Old Testament? How is He recognised in the life of a believer? Is His presence IN a believer the same as His presence UPON a believer? Is speaking in tongues really necessary? This book on spiritual warfare emphasises the role of the Holy Spirit in the Old and New testaments.

## WHEN TWO HALVES MAKE A HOLE

Behind every broken marriage is a fierce battle that was lost in the spiritual realm. Many people do not realise that from the moment they say "I do" a raging battle starts whose sole objective is the break-up of their marriage. The Bible warns us that our enemy the devil prowls around like a roaring Lion looking for someone to devour. We are told not to be passive a onlooker but to "Resist him..." Thus the battle for our marriage is not an option but a command.

## Other Books by Author

### UNGODLY SOUL TIES

Did you know that there are relationships that we walked away from as many as ten years ago that can still keep us in bondage? Many people are not aware that the way they behave today may be directly related to the way their parents, or even a kindergarten teacher treated them in childhood. Ungodly soul ties are often forged between us by people who have abused us physically, emotionally or psychologically. This book will tell you how to identify and break them through the power of the cross of Jesus Christ.

### BREAKING FINANCIAL CURSES

Since it is God's desire to give generously to His children, why are so many of His children languishing in poverty? Jesus said that He came so that we may have abundant life. Abundance is not going to bed hungry, or not being able to pay for my children's education, or not having house-rent. Abundance is being amply supplied for by my heavenly Father! 2 Corinthians 9:8 says, "And God is able to make all grace abound to you, so that in all things at all times, having all that you need, you will abound in every good work." This book attempts to identify some of the barriers that may be standing in the way of many well-meaning and diligent Christians.

www.ingramcontent.com/pod-product-compliance
Lightning Source LLC
Chambersburg PA
CBHW070856050426
42453CB00012B/2236